ONE
MOOR
TIME

For Mum & Dad, who first took me
walking on the moors

For Siân, who continues to walk there
with me now

Crumps Barn Studio
Syde, Cheltenham GL53 9PN
www.crumpsbarnstudio.co.uk

Copyright © Ben Pering 2024
First printed 2024
Reprinted 2025

The right of Ben Pering to be identified as the author of this work has been
asserted in accordance with the Copyright, Designs and Patents Act 1988.

Cover design by Lorna Gray
Cover artwork and illustrations © Molly Brown www.mollybrown.ink
Photograph © the author

Typeset in Adobe Garamond Pro

All our books are printed on responsibly sourced paper from managed woodlands.
Printed in the UK by CMP, Poole.

ISBN 978-1-915067-61-6

ONE MOOR TIME

BEN PERING

*A tale of four enthusiastic yet misguided attempts
to walk the* Two Moors Way

Crumps Barn Studio

PROLOGUE

THERE ARE THREE OF US in the back seat, squeezed in shoulder to shoulder, wearing brand new school uniforms.

My dad has done the rounds to collect two of my friends so he can take us all together to our very first day of secondary school. We are eleven years old, and we are incredibly nervous.

The old car putters up the hill slowly and my dad natters in the driver's seat; he is talking to us, but he's mostly just trying to fill the awkward silence and lighten the mood. As we crest the brow of the suburban hill, we can see the unmistakable shape of Dartmoor on the horizon, with its swooping valleys and iconic craggy peaks.

I have known this view my whole life. It's always been there – another world in the near distance. We would regularly head up to the moor at weekends and during holidays to explore the woods and hills and rivers and wildlife. To this day, its ancient, knotty environments represent escape to me, a way to step outside of life's mundanity to find freedom and adventure.

From the back seat of the car, I nervously ask my dad if he fancies heading up that way today, instead of taking us to school.

He smiles, and for a split second I think he probably even considers it.

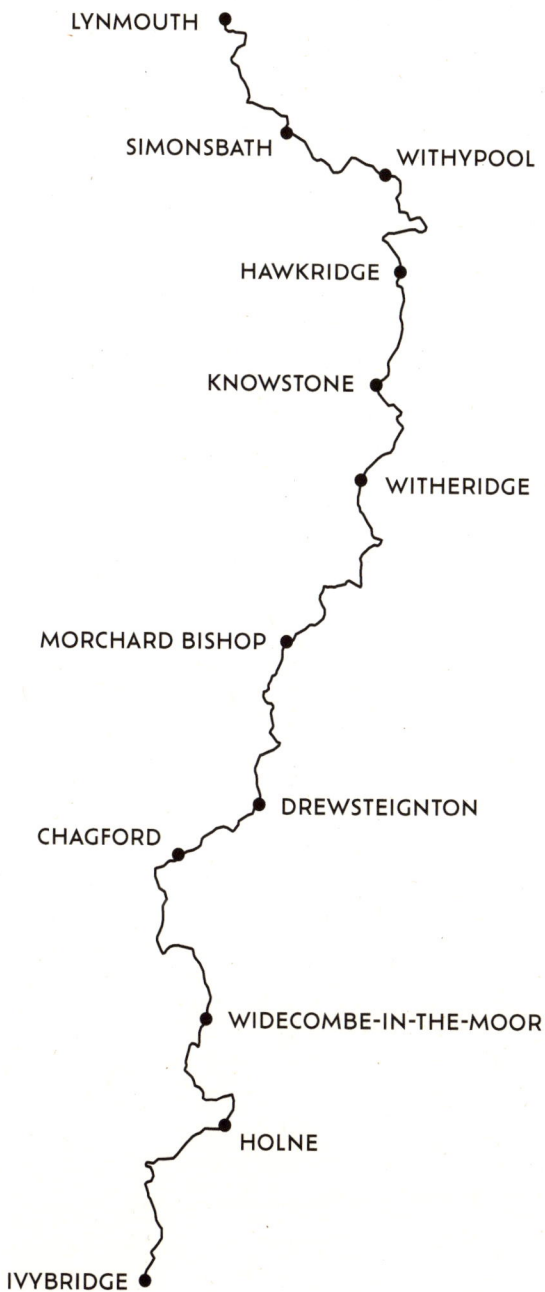

LYNMOUTH

SIMONSBATH

WITHYPOOL

HAWKRIDGE

KNOWSTONE

WITHERIDGE

MORCHARD BISHOP

DREWSTEIGNTON

CHAGFORD

WIDECOMBE-IN-THE-MOOR

HOLNE

IVYBRIDGE

FIRST ATTEMPT

'Every time we turn around to look back at where we've come from, we find we've ascended a little further into the heavens, seeing the swathes of green farm fields splaying out across the South Devon landscape below'

I ONLY TOOK TWO PHOTOGRAPHS the first time. One was right at the very start, on the southern edge of Dartmoor. After a brief walk from Ivybridge train station, the leafy suburban side road offers up a right turn over a stone bridge that crosses the railway line and heads out of town. The slope of the moor rises up beyond the scrabbly roadside bushes and trees, beckoning solemnly as they sway in the wind. That smooth dome of moorland hillside is so imposing it almost looks like some alien planet appearing in orbit for the first time. And right there at the side of the railway bridge, mounted on a granite boulder the size of a giant's fist, is the Dartmoor National Park logo. It shows a white horse with flowing mane, unhindered as it runs free in the ancient and unspoiled wilds. A perfect scene to be the first photograph of an epic and adventure-filled hike.

The only other photo I ended up taking on that cheap disposable camera came about thirty seconds later, at the exact same spot. My friend Sam, his foot up on the boulder, all stocky shoulders and hirsute legs, hair and beard ratty and bleached in the sun. He looked very much like a young hobbit who had recently discovered the joys of surfing.

Sam and I first met at school when we both lived

in Devon and so we both knew Dartmoor well. In our early twenties we found ourselves both living and attending university in Bristol. Sam was very much built to walk long distances – the hobbit-like appearance was no accident. He was sturdy, rugged, and steadfast in his demeanour. With his leg up on that Dartmoor National Park sign, he looked every inch a young man ready to take on a week-long hike with ease.

As those were the only photographs I ended up taking on our trip, I have no record of my outward appearance on that day, but to be honest the chances are I was likely still hungover from whatever I'd been up to the night before. I was twenty-two years old – an irresponsible leaf in a stream, just doing whatever came my way with the vague certainty that it would probably all work out somehow. I don't remember the exact conversation that had led us to this point, but it very likely consisted of Sam saying "Hey, do you want to walk the Two Moors Way?" and me saying "Sure, why not?" and then just going along with it because, well … sure, why not. I didn't know the way, I didn't have a map, I didn't have much of a clue of what I was letting myself in for.

I did know where Dartmoor was, which I suppose was something. I had some old walking boots, a pair of *solar dry* trousers*, and a ratty old rucksack into which Sam had stuffed half his tent, some rice and a bottle of

---

* Seriously, they had a special tag on the side actually advertising their unique ability to dry in the sun…

water. I then added the disposable camera, an old, blunt pen knife, a sleeping bag, and a couple of pairs of socks. Those were the kinds of things people took hiking, right?

It took many years for those photos to eventually see the light of day, as that particular camera fell into a time vortex in the bottom of a desk drawer somewhere. Eventually sidelined by the advent of digital cameras and smartphone whatsappsnapchattery, quaint notions like disposable cameras soon became nostalgic oddities that only appeared at kitschy weddings or themed New Year's Eve parties. Clearly at some point I must've stumbled across this one when moving house and decided to see what treasures it contained. And there they were: two grainy, dark, but immediately recognisable photos, recalling two young friends just setting off on their adventure – one ready for anything, the other wielding a disposable camera and a cheap rucksack full of next-to-nothing.

After crossing the railway out of Ivybridge, the road becomes narrow as it starts to snake up to meet the broad shoulders of Butterdon Hill. After a spell it turns into a rocky track that soon becomes a dried-up streambed that then spits you out into the relative emptiness of the moor above. The bushes and fences that guided you so directly until that point cease abruptly, depositing you at the foot of an endless sea of shorn, browning grass, earthen red bracken, and piles of hard, grey stone jutting like exposed bones through the soft fleshy ground. It seems to rise up forever and outwards in all directions, the bush-bound path you've just been walking now cast as a tiny tributary emptying into a vast estuary of open moorland.

This climb is one of those that feels like it goes on forever – whenever it seems like you're getting to the crest of something, somehow another fresh hilltop appears on the horizon just to taunt you. Yet Sam and I are fresh and confident on the first leg of our first day walking and we're happy to keep climbing. Every time we turn around to look back at where we've come from, we find we've ascended a little further into the heavens, seeing the swathes of green farm fields splaying out across the South Devon landscape below, dotted with little villages and towns, and the shining slivers of ever-widening rivers shattering the view like a cracks in a pane of glass. There, in the far distance, lies Plymouth, squatting like a dog at the foot of the Tamar River. It almost looks pleasant from so far away.

Southern Dartmoor has a very different character to what locals affectionately call *the tourist moor* – the twisty lanes and roughly farmed fields that surround the busy village of Widecombe, beautiful and welcoming, like stepping back in time yet somehow also entirely timeless. Those wooded cleaves of East Dartmoor are all bubbly hedges and lush greenery, studded with open heaths and peaked with recognisable tors, like little beacons all around.

The Southern Moor, on the other hand, is an ocean of empty, rolling hillsides with very little to differentiate each one from the next, other than the particular patchwork of green, red, and beige mottling caused by the grass, bracken, and bare earth vying for position.

The first day of the Two Moors Way winds up and around these rolling hills for a good ten miles, offering a fairly simple track to follow that finally reaches the top of the ridge. There it wriggles around the contours of various tors and valleys as it heads north. We have the weather on our side and we make good time, eventually stopping by a long-abandoned quarry site for our lunch. On the path a little stone bridge separates a dug-out hole now filled with water, and an equally sized artificial hillock, speckled with rocks and weeds. Whilst it has clearly stood like this for at least a hundred years, the small scale of the mound and pond already strikes us as strangely man-made, after a morning spent adjusting to the natural vastness of our surroundings. It doesn't take long for the open moor to work its magic.

As that feeling begins to grow, we settle into an easy gait and we talk about our lives. We are both young men. Life is yet unformed for us, and we are still bursting with possibility. We are both in youthful relationships – with all their attendant highs and dramatic complications. We discuss the details like they're Shakespearean plays. We have vague plans and unsighted ambitions, with an over-inflated sense of their importance to the world. Sam is finishing up his music degree; I've recently re-started a degree in music technology, after having dropped out a couple of years earlier. I like to imagine myself as deep and complex, but in truth I am an uncomplicated soul – I like good pubs and loud music and doing things with friends that feel unplanned (without yet realising that those things that feel unplanned have, in reality, just been planned by someone else, someone far more responsible). Neither of us has yet laid out those unyielding tracks that our adult lives will eventually run on, and so we walk together and we discuss ourselves and our juvenile philosophies in the way that young men will often only do when they're unburdened and active out in the world together.

Eventually we begin to descend again, into the Avon Valley. The presence of water alters the otherwise bleak, parched nature of the moorland. The river is at a low ebb as we're in mid-summer – but the immediate freshness to the air and the magical dance of sound that comes from cool water finding its way through strewn rocks is delightful. I'm very happy to take the chance to rest on the bank awhile, but am soon aware that the day is pressing on and we still have a fair way to go. After bounding across a few choice boulders, we follow the far bank downstream before peeling away on the north-easterly bearing that should take us on towards the slow rise of Pupers Hill.

A little way into the ascent, it becomes fairly clear that we've managed to lose the track. We soon find ourselves waist deep in tussocks, every step laboured and deeply aggravating – every moor walker knows the joys of tussocky ground. Each footfall is a potential ankle breaker, or knee cruncher, or sudden waist-deep bog seemingly just the width of your leg and no more.

A glance around suggests no alternative route, so we press on – climbing upwards in the general direction we should be moving and just hoping the path will reappear to us soon.

It doesn't. For the next hour I drag myself up and up, following Sam through endless tussocks that alternate between bone-crunchingly shallow or inexplicably fathoms deep. On terrain like this every footstep is a lottery and I find myself fast losing my patience. This should probably have been a twenty minute climb, but instead we seem to have found ourselves in a new circle of hell: one previously missed by Dante. I quickly become tired, grumpy, and thirsty. As the sun recedes the midges join in the party, skimming and whizzing around our heads and then making kamikaze attacks at the worst moment, just to add an insult to every injury inflicted by the uneven ground. It's at this point it really dawns on me just how woefully ill-equipped and under-prepared I am for all this. I am not happy.

After a fraught eternity we reach the top of the hill, the tussocks giving way to just regular old uneven grassy ground, and we see the path we lost some way off to our right. We steer ourselves back towards it, but my cheerful demeanour has long since faded, and I huff and puff my way back down the far side of the hill. This is all Sam's fault – of course. It's not like I know the way or anything, is it? How could he have got us so lost? How irresponsible.

The next stretch of the walk that skirts the far side of Pupers Hill and drops down to Chalk Ford on the edge of Buckfastleigh Moor is a particularly beautiful section, all tumbling gorse thickets and solitary, ancient oaks. I'm not paying attention to any of that though. I am trudging.

We arrive in the small farming village of Scorriton a couple of hours later. The path off of the open moor that leads into the village is vague in my memory: a blur of rocky, ankle bending scree, camouflaged against the meandering track by the darkening sky above the trees. The sun is starting to hide behind the surrounding hills, giving the village a half-lit ambience and making the warm glow from the pub windows seem like the most appealing thing in the world. I want to dive inside and immediately drink five pints, but Sam insists we continue on to Holne, the next village about thirty minutes further down the lanes. I protest for a while, but there's a pub there too so eventually I cave and go along with it.

The Church House Inn in Holne is a beautiful, ancient watering hole, full of dark oak beams and private nooks into which a tired walker can deposit themselves to refuel with a drink. The moment a pint passes my lips I feel immediately better. Sam is keen to drink up and get the tent pitched before dark, but I'm having none of it – I drink a second pint to wash down a bag of pork scratchings and feel all the life return to my body. I fully believe that sitting in a pub with a quality pint of ale at the end of a long walk is one of the finest things a person can do for themselves. Now with two pints inside me, I tell Sam about this at great length.

Eventually though, Sam wins out with all his common sense and forward planning, and we exile ourselves from the warm embrace of the pub and back into the cool of the summer evening. We walk out of the village a little way and climb a stile into an empty field, where we pitch the tent and light the Trangia stove. Sam's tent isn't really a two man tent, it's a one man with a bit of bonus room for a large pack, but we're friends and so we're fine to make do. We eat lukewarm rice with a spoonful of pesto and then bed down for the night. I sleep like a baby.

There are many, many breathtaking stretches over the course of the hundred mile trail that runs from Ivybridge to Lynmouth. The walk from Holne that chases and joins the River Dart as it winds towards Spitchwick is one of them – the sun-dappled woodland dropping away to reveal the glorious sweep of the river below, its rushing waters alternating between deep, clear, earthen brown pools and then brilliant white froth as it rushes over the granite rocks that narrow it into channels that surge back into even deeper, swirling pools. The path drops down the side of the valley, drawing closer to the joyous swirl of the water, as it wills you ever onward alongside it. At Spitchwick the pace slows and the river meanders out wide. It creates a perfect grassy green plateau, wrapped in a gentle band of flowing water and backed by sheer cliffs topped with trees that seem like they're peering over the edge of some ancient fortification.

It's not long after sunrise – we packed up and set off as soon as the tent was too airless and uncomfortable to continue sleeping – yet there are already other people here: morning swimmers in the deepest part of the channel where their feet can't touch the rocky bottom, their dogs splashing happily nearby in the shallows.

As we linger by the water, I begin to notice the dark clouds approach. Despite a cool, dry night, the morning has crawled in muggy and slightly overcast. This morning murk isn't unusual for a British summer, but instead of burning off to reveal another scorching day, there's something slightly more sinister appearing on the horizon. We pull out our waterproof jackets as the first heavy drops begin to fall, and we immediately duck back into the woods for some cover. It doesn't help though – the next few hours of walking are up the exposed side of Newbridge Hill, into which the bruised, coalescing clouds empty their payload in an unbroken torrent.

We join the road, abandoning the overgrown, zig-zag-ging path in order to try and march up the hill as quickly as we can, but soon the road swings away from us and we're back on the increasingly muddy track, trudging through waist high foliage with our coat hoods pulled tight around our noses. The endless bracken that sprawls across the hillside has recently been burned in a con-trolled fire. It gives the ascent a strange, alien quality – we are surrounded by knots of angular, blackened sinew, and faced with a marble grey sky that just wants to see us drowned. The full ascent up Dr Blackall's Drive to Bel Tor car park takes about two hours; we push on without stopping for the whole thing, mostly because there would be little rest to be gained without any shelter. At the very top the rain finally breaks and the clouds start to part. It feels like we've just run a gauntlet set by Old Crockern himself, and it's only 10am.

The sun resumes service as we gladly strip off our sweat-soaked waterproofs and strap them to the outsides of our rucksacks to get dry. It's downhill all the way to the little hamlet of Ponsworthy from here, and we're flanked by Dartmoor ponies, grazing on grass and moss from between the littered boulders and the crumbling dry stone walls that guide our journey down. We refill our water bottles at the spring there and decide to take a detour from the trail and head to Widecombe for lunch. Following the lane into the village is a strange feeling after so much time spent on rough tracks, and the bush-bound tarmac offered up by the lanes seems a little disappointing.

Widecombe is as beautiful as ever though, all picture-perfect cottages enfolded in the sweeping curve of the valley. We set ourselves down on a table outside The Wayside Café and order a cream tea. It arrives on a plastic tray, fat scones still bulging with fresh steam and little pots overflowing with jam and clotted cream. It's a glorious sight to behold. A proper Devonshire cream tea isn't some fancy lace doily affair, no delicate fruit arrangement or sprinkled powdered sugar. Instead, it's honest, rustic, fresh – just bursting at the seams with way too much of everything – and yet somehow you can still manage to consume every last mouthful before you pop. Of course, it's essential to wash it all down with a cup of strong tea poured out of some ancient china teapot, most likely adorned with watercolour paintings of beagles or meandering rivers. No one knows where these teapots come from, but it seems they will endure forever.

The only thing anyone really ever needs after eating an entire cream tea is a four hour nap, but to my great disappointment, we don't have time for such a luxury. Heading north out of Widecombe, the path lurches back off the road and straight up the steep side of Hameldown – a long, supine ridge that rolls and rises up like the chest of a slumbering giant. Once up onto the ridge itself, it's a long, steady ascent to the highest point in the entire hundred mile route: Hameldown Beacon. The three hundred and sixty degree views from every point on the ridge are prime Dartmoor, but from the Beacon itself you can see what feels like the entirety of Devon; the swooping hills eventually giving way to hazy farmland, with the slick sheen of the sea in the far distance.

It's a sharp drop from there down to the prehistoric settlement of Grimspound, a dramatic and impressive stone ring that was long ago used for penning livestock and protecting their isolated community from the elements. The sugar rush of the cream tea has long since worn off and I'm feeling the day begin to drag, and so we take a westerly track that leads off the main route, which we know will take us on a welcome detour to the Warren House Inn.

Rolling through the bracken studded hills, the land here looks like it's been scarred by a huge knife, or perhaps ploughed by the same giant we've just traversed the length of. Great furrows of bare earth split the hillside in two, and Sam and I walk alongside them wondering what could have caused such unnatural wounds to open up in the flesh of the land itself. The answer is, of course, some kind of quarrying or mining activity that's gone on in the past, but such surroundings don't lend themselves to that kind of mundane sensibility.

The Warren House Inn is definitely one of the best pubs in the country, possibly the world. Perched high and lonely on the side of the road that runs from Princetown to Moretonhampstead, it's a haven of good food and well-kept beer that is entirely ensconced in the majesty of the landscape around it, its plaster-white walls propping up a mess of thatch and an ever-billowing chimney that acts as a beacon to walkers for miles around. The fire inside is said to have been burning continuously since 1845 – whether this is true or not is a point of conjecture, but either way the bar is stocked with local ales and the tables out the front sit above the sweep of the valley below, creating the perfect vantage to view the moor for miles.

We head into the welcome warmth and fetch ourselves some well-earned pints, before marching back outside to sit at a table and stare out at that view. I can see the spine of Hameldown forming the horizon, as well as the drop down to Grimspound, the settlement appearing as an almost perfect grey circle from this distance. It's most likely my insistence that brings about our second pints, but in a place like this it's hard to resist. We are wary about staying too long though, as the shadows are starting to grow long and we still have several miles to go before we get to Chagford, our stop-off for the night.

It may be the beer, or perhaps the desire to make up for lost time (or maybe both), but after shouldering our packs and dropping our used glasses back to the bar, we decide that we should run to the top of Chagford common – the long, grassy plateau that extends from behind the pub to the eastern edge of Fernworthy Forest to the north. The sun is beginning to drop behind the far side, so in a fit of spontaneity we start to run straight up the ragged, steep hillside directly behind the pub. There is no path, we're just picking whichever route through the knotty foliage seems as direct as possible, trying to make it to the top first. As the slope flattens out at the plateau crest, we meet the sun again, breathless and laughing and ready to begin the final stage of the day's walk.

As we set off again, I immediately notice a twinge in my right knee. Half an hour later, it's a sharp, throbbing pain. By the time we're walking off the common and entering the lanes that will wind for a mile or two into Chagford, I am slowed to a crawl. The last mile takes us an hour to walk, Sam propping me up as my swelling knee refuses to bend. It's fully dark by the time we arrive in the centre of the village, and I can no longer support any weight on my leg. We drop into The Ring of Bells – one of the three pubs on offer – and order some crisps and water to a table that I can sit next to with my leg raised. Sam heads back out into the night to find somewhere to pitch the tent. He returns not long later and informs me he's found somewhere, but we'll need to wait here until closing time. I feel slightly woozy from pain and hunger, but I'm more than happy to stuff myself with crisps and sink another pint for the time being.

At 11pm the pub closes, and we lurch out of the door into the cool of the night. Sam has managed to shoulder both our packs and I've picked up some long-abandoned walking pole from behind the bar to support myself with. Just around the corner is the church, the iron gates unlocked and the yard hemmed in by tall trees and waist high walls. I plonk myself gracelessly onto the mossy ground with my leg stuck out straight in front of me. Sam pitches the tent as I fumble with the Trangia stove. Eventually we summon some more rice and pesto and then I struggle into my sleeping bag. Neither of us are sure if it's acceptable to camp in a churchyard, but given the situation there aren't really any other good options. We talk about how a good night's sleep will fix whatever I've done to myself with a cautious optimism, but I can feel that the pain in my leg isn't just a minor issue. We crawl back into the tiny tent and hope for sleep to work its magic.

It turns out to be one of the worst night's sleep I've ever had. Somehow, in spite of being mid-summer, the temperature plummets. I lie in my sleeping bag, shivering. The shivering causes my leg to tense and stiffen, sending a shard of pain coursing through me, causing my whole body to clench up. Eventually it recedes and I manage to relax my body again, just enough to begin to fall asleep. At that moment of relaxation the cold hits me, and I start to shiver again. I repeat this cycle for hours; alternating between cold, pain, and a maddening state of almost sleep. As is always the case with a bad night's sleep, by 4am I'm so exhausted that sleep overcomes me anyway, before I awake what feels like seconds later to the sound of the iron gate being pushed open and the light of dawn creeping into the tent. Sam leaps up to greet whoever has entered the churchyard, to assure them we mean no harm and explain away the situation. After they've gone, I drag myself out of the tent and then out of my sleeping bag like a snake shedding its skin. My knee is swollen and wracked with pain whenever it is moved. It is pretty clear I'm not walking anywhere else for a while.

After a rustling up some porridge on the stove, Sam takes down the tent and we stash our bags against the wall, so as to look as innocuous as possible. We wait until the day has fully begun and the shops are starting to open, before doing what any foolish young man does when they find themselves in a bind.

I call my dad.

He may roll his eyes about things like this, but the truth is that there is nothing my dad likes more than jumping in his Land Rover and belting up to Dartmoor to come to the rescue. Unfortunately, it is midweek and like most sensible people he is at work and wouldn't be able to get there until after 6pm. We'd need to wait in Chagford for the day.

Fortunately, Chagford has three very nice pubs, and from the moment they opened for business we availed ourselves of the lot, moving between them periodically and passing the time with a few pints, some card games, and a lot of packets of crisps. By the time we were finally rescued we'd both had enough of a skinful that we weren't really thinking about the fact that we'd had to abandon the walk we'd set out on just two days earlier.

That creeping feeling of failure would come later.

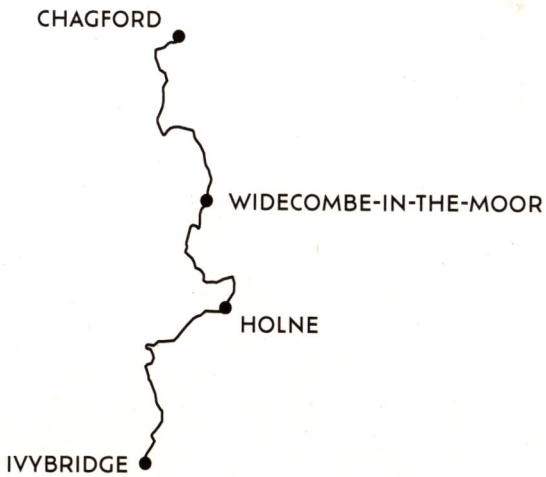

CHAGFORD

WIDECOMBE-IN-THE-MOOR

HOLNE

IVYBRIDGE

SECOND ATTEMPT

*'The track is slowly swallowed by a sea of long grass,
and try as we might, it seems like no change of
direction will bring us back to it'*

LESS THAN A YEAR LATER, I would find myself getting off the train at Ivybridge again, standing beside Sam, packs on our backs and ready to go. This time I was more prepared and I'd been far more involved in the planning process. When I say "far more involved", what I really mean is that I'd been the one who suggested we try to do it again. Whereas before I'd just tagged along for kicks, this time I had a drive of my own: a vision of getting to the end and making up for the previous year's defeat. This time I had something to prove.

On top of that, the last ten months hadn't been among my best. I'd been wallowing in a heartbreak I didn't have the emotional maturity to deal with, I'd let many things slip in my life, and had wound up profoundly stuck in a rut. The idea of getting back out into the wild and having another go at the walk that beat me was something I felt I needed; a feeling of achievement that might reinvigorate me. It also coincided nicely with the annual festival at Lynmouth that our group of friends had taken to visiting each year, although this time the plan was that Sam and I would be arriving on foot. I anticipated a heroic and victorious arrival after finishing our epic quest, being carried to the beach on the shoulders of an awed and impressed throng of friends, now fully ready for a good party and for all my troubles to instantly become a distant memory.

And so there we were at the Dartmoor National Park sign again, only this time in pelting rain. We had our game faces on – we needed to be in Lynmouth in five days' time, so we had to make good on each day's walking. No photographs this time, but straight up the side of Butterdon Hill, waterproofs on and heads looking down as we marched. Last time we'd strolled across the open ridge in the sun talking about our lives, relationships, and plans; this time we discussed heartbreak and failure from within the confines of our hoods. The tone was different. We were different.

We wound our way through the rolling hilltops in a rain-soaked haze. Walking in the rain forced us into a trudge – I hunch my head forward to pull my hood in front of my brow, taking tighter steps to avoid slipping in the slick mud underfoot. Our conversation was bleaker and more subdued than the previous year: I was struggling with the second year of my degree – the need to take it seriously and knuckle down still rubbing up against my reflexive indifference. Not only did completing this walk promise the catharsis I hugely needed, it also represented a change I craved in myself, a resilience and capacity to stick with something to the end. I wanted to become someone new, someone who could take what was thrown at me and run with it. What had been an adventure undertaken on a whim last year was now a symbol of the change I wanted to see in myself but was struggling to grasp.

In spite of this desire for change, I had all the exact same gear as last time – the same *solar dry* trousers[*], the same boots, backpack, and sleeping bag. This time I'd also bought a first aid kit, some spare t-shirts, socks and underpants, and enough snack bars to last a month. This might not sound like much, but compared to the previous year I was kitted out and ready for whatever the journey might throw at me. We also had a slightly larger tent this time, as our friend George was planning to join us on the third day and we'd need the extra space. The first two nights were going to be luxuriously roomy though.

The rain eases off as we cross the Avon River, although the water level is notably higher than before and crossing proves trickier. We remember The Scaling of the Hill From Hell where we ended up losing our way and our sanity last time, so try to keep to the path as best we can – but to no avail. The track is slowly swallowed by a sea of long grass, and try as we might, it seems like no change of direction will bring us back to it. Once again the desperation rises as I find myself knee high in tussocks that want to break my ankles and then drag me

---

[*] Honestly, the guy that sold them to me in Millets made it sound like an incredible technological innovation.

down beneath the surface of the earth for good measure.

We eventually make it to Holne again though, and enjoy ourselves a well-earned pint before heading over to the field we'd camped in before. The sense of adventure and exploration we'd shared last year is missing, but I knew we had to crack on through the first two days to get to some fresh walking routes again. It would be worth it.

The next day the weather holds fast and we make good time. As before, we detour to Widecombe for lunch, but also to pull out our primitive mobile phones so we can find enough signal to check in with George. He would be getting into Exeter that afternoon, and could then jump on a bus to somewhere on the route – we just need to work out where. As I study the map, a problem occurs to me. At the pace we're currently walking, there is almost no chance we're going to make it to Lynmouth in just five days.

Sam and I discuss this for a while. Our goals here are twofold: to complete the walk we'd challenged ourselves to defeat, and to make it to the festival to be with our friends and enjoy the reward of some well-earned summer hedonism. If we were going to make it to the festival in time, then we would need to skip a day's walk. Sam touts a plan that involves getting the bus from Widecombe to Exeter, meeting up with George there, and then taking another bus to the end point of what should be the third day at Morchard Bishop. We would then be ready to set off fresh in the morning to walk what should've been day four, putting us a day ahead of schedule and on track to arrive in time.

This seems sensible, but disappointing. For my part, I really want to complete the whole route – but my youthful joie de vivre can't pass up the opportunity to party, and what better way to enter a party than arriving at the end of a hike? Really, what would even be the point of walking all this way if we miss the party at the end? Would it actually matter if we skipped a day …?

In this manner I eventually talked myself into the idea that getting to the end was more important than the journey itself. Wiser folk know there's probably a lesson to be taken from that, but it would be many years before I'd get there myself. In hindsight, we really should've noticed the timing mistake long before we ever set off on this walk. If only someone was paying attention to these things – it was probably Sam's fault, somehow.

We get on the bus and ride up out of Widecombe, looking out across the moorland surrounds through smeary windows. The route back to civilisation takes us past Haytor, its huge stone prominence protruding out of the ground like a fist, studded with tourists and dog walkers and climbers with all their gear. We feel like tourists too now; no longer intrepid explorers but mere day-trippers getting the bus back to the city. Arriving into the centre of Exeter is a strange sensation; to have gone from such vast, ancient surrounds to the graffiti tinged confines of the angular, concrete city is jarring. We wait for George to arrive and then quickly get on the bus that will take us to Morchard Bishop.

George is clearly feeling fresh and in good spirits, obviously enjoying that the bus is taking him out towards adventure. That attitude is infectious and we soon get our enthusiasm for walking back, telling ourselves that missing a section of the route isn't all that bad. Arriving in the small village of Morchard Bishop at about 3pm, we decide not to tarry but to crack on and gain ourselves some ground. We fill up our water bottles at the village shop and immediately set out.

The Two Moors Way has three distinct sections. The first is across Dartmoor, starting in Ivybridge, stopping overnight in Holne, continuing to Chagford and then crossing off the moor just north of Drewsteignton. Dartmoor is rolling and vast, but interspersed with wooded valleys and quiet trickling streams, all rugged beauty and permeated with the feeling of ancient life.

The second section really begins once you cross the A30, as after that you're properly into mid Devon. No longer ancient and wild, mid Devon is a rustic sprawl of pastoral farmland, perfectly round, copse-topped hills, and tiny, picturesque villages. The path constantly switches between country lanes, rocky tracks, and long stretches of patchworked fields where walkers need to stay in close to the bushes to avoid disturbing whatever livestock make their home there. It stops in at Morchard Bishop, Witheridge, and Knowstone along the way as it winds north.

The final section is across Exmoor, which is smaller and less grandiose than Dartmoor, but in some ways much bleaker. There are less signs of that timeless beauty, and more long, windswept, bracken filled ridges, slashed deep with steep, craggy valleys. The trail from Hawkridge to Simonsbath follows a beautiful stretch of the River Barle; but it's the northern coast at Lynmouth where the trail comes to its end that is truly spectacular, and in my mind is the key reason why the walk should be done from south to north.

Morchard Bishop is slap bang in the middle of the mid Devon leg. On paper, this section is easier going; less altitude to be gained and less rough terrain underfoot – but in reality, it's hampered by unkempt tracks, the constant up and down of the smaller but steep little hills, and much more complex navigating. We spend a lot of time doubling back on ourselves to find the path, and sweeping huge fields to figure out which gate we're meant to be leaving through.

George is a tall, slim, athletic man – standing an easy half foot taller than both Sam and I – and he seems to be made almost entirely of leg. He has a mop of bright red hair covering his good-natured face, and a very direct enthusiasm that allows no time for any moping around.

He sets off at an intimidating pace. Sam, of course, is still a natural born walker and he happily keeps up. I gamely up my speed to match, but now that George is pace-setting I begin to find the afternoon's walking tough going. By the time we arrive in Knowstone that night, I am very chafed.

Chafing is a well-known problem for walkers, but not something that gets a great deal of literature written about it. There are a great many volumes written on *The Various Joys of Walking in Nature*, or *The Mysterious Allure of Some Ancient Pathway*, but I've yet to come across a book called *Times My Undercarriage Got So Badly Chafed I Had to Give Up and Go Home.*[*] This is in part because there are some fairly straightforward preventative measures that can be taken, and any serious walker is likely long past the point where it's still an issue.

As expected though, I have considered none of those things. My *solar dry* trousers are a bit snug after a year of eating my feelings, and my cheap boxer shorts are thin and full of holes. I waddle into Knowstone that evening several minutes behind Sam and George, in pretty bad shape.

Knowstone is a tiny village, but it does have The Masons Arms, a lovely pub right in the centre. We set ourselves up with pints and crisps as we try to figure out where to pitch the tent that evening. We'll need to head back out of the village to find a field, but at this

---

* I am noting it down as the title of my follow up though.

point I am really not at all equipped to walk any further. After a while I suggest we ask if they'll let us camp in the beer garden, once they've closed for the night. I am mostly up for this because it means we get to stay in the pub until closing time, but it also does seem to make sense. George heads off to the bar to ask, and the very friendly and accommodating staff agree. We nurse pints until 11pm, then once the place is locked up, we crack out the tent.

Having now drunk a good four pints, I have forgotten all about my sore thighs and I'm very ready to sleep. We all squeeze ourselves into the very tight tent and within minutes I begin to snore outrageously. Every few minutes I get woken from my reverie by an elbow to the ribs, only to roll over and begin snoring again.

No one sleeps well that night. We crawl out of the tent at first light, feeling neither refreshed nor rested.

I begin the day by stuffing cotton wool and a mess of plasters into the narrow gap between my scorched thighs and my trousers. We have two more days of hard walking ahead of us to get to Lynmouth and the sweet feeling of victory it promises, so my only option is to find a solution that makes it vaguely bearable. I throw some painkillers into my porridge and shoulder my rucksack, ready to give it my best shot.

This impromptu solution does reduce the soreness,

but very much adds to the John Wayne-style waddle. I was the slowest of the three of us already, but now I am hobbled even further. I spend most of the day just trying to keep up, and it sucks all of the joy out of another beautiful stretch of the trail. After leaving Knowstone, the landscape slowly changes again as the path winds through the southern foothills of Exmoor. Villages and roads become fewer, paths and hedgerows become increasingly unkempt. After a few miles, we meet the rise of Exmoor as it slopes up into infinity. As we ascend, the surrounding landscape shifts from green to brown once again – dense hedgerows full of life being displaced by knotty clumps of sun-beaten gorse and heather, the ever-present bracken carpet filling in the gaps.

As we slowly approach Withypool, I spend the afternoon getting increasingly exhausted as I trudge forward with an unnatural gait in an attempt to avoid the pain in my scoured thighs. My enthusiasm wanes as Sam and George have to repeatedly stop and wait for me to catch up whenever I fall too far behind, the concern etched on their faces increasing each time. I press on with all the grit I can muster, determined to earn the catharsis I had coming at the end of this endurance test, but by the time we arrive at The Royal Oak that evening I'm shattered. The customary pints and crisps are inhaled once again to try and glean some of their restorative powers as fast as I can, but even that isn't enough to bring me back to life. Some friends of ours arrive at the pub soon after with a plan to join us for dinner on their way to the festival by car. It doesn't take long to decide that I should jump in with them and let Sam and George finish the final day of the walk themselves. They bid me their apologetic good-byes and then set off again in order to use the remaining daylight to get to Simonsbath. Not long after, I leave with the others by car.

I sit slumped in the backseat as we twist down the windy lanes towards Lynmouth. Soon the tiredness I feel is joined by a sadness that washes over me like a wave – I have failed once again, and due to my own lack of preparation and ability, no less. I couldn't blame it on a freak knee sprain this time; instead I'm forced to admit that the Two Moors Way is just too much for me. It doesn't feel good.

To add insult to injury, the next morning I awoke in a tent in Lynmouth to the sound of Sam and George arriving on foot – they'd set off nice and early and made excellent time, arriving at the finish line only a few hours later. Sam described the route to me and told me it was such a straight-forward walk I probably could've managed it if I'd stayed with them. I tried to reassure myself with the knowledge that none of us actually completed the whole route and even if I had stuck out the last day with them it still would only have been a partial finish. Regardless, the sense of completion and achievement I'd' been craving when we set out this time still eluded me.

Yet the festival itself was, as always, a delightful occasion. I managed to shake off some of the despondency I was feeling with a sunny blend of music, beer, good company, and incredible surroundings. I headed home a few days later feeling refreshed in spite of a second failed attempt, and as time passed I began to think of walking the Two Moors Way as something that had just been a missed opportunity. I began to believe I wasn't capable and perhaps never would be – and that it would forever remain something I had tried and failed to achieve, and that maybe I just wasn't cut out for it in the first place. Life moved on, as it always does – and this is how I would continue to think about it for a long time.

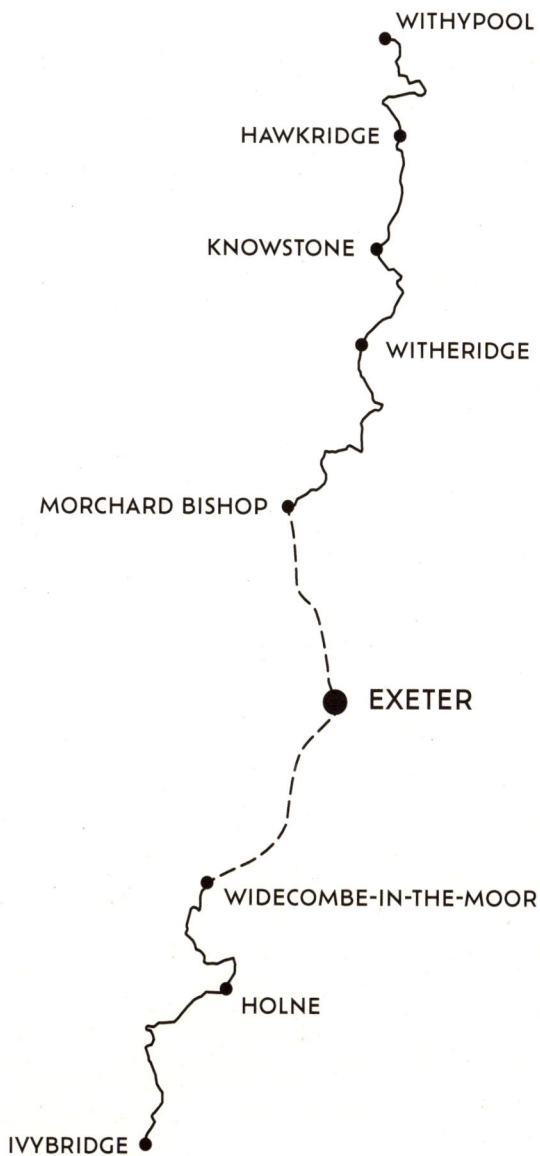

WITHYPOOL

HAWKRIDGE

KNOWSTONE

WITHERIDGE

MORCHARD BISHOP

EXETER

WIDECOMBE-IN-THE-MOOR

HOLNE

IVYBRIDGE

TEN YEARS

'Always making sure to end a good day's walking with a pint of fine ale and a packet of salty crisps'

ONCE THAT DISASTROUS SECOND ATTEMPT had faded into the past, I didn't think about trying again. It just seemed like a done deal after how poorly I'd fared on the second attempt – I told myself it just wasn't the sort of thing I was cut out for, but convinced myself that I'd given it my best shot and that that was that.

That being said, the memories of those two hikes stayed around in my mind for a long time. There were several stretches that had awed me with their beauty, and I returned to them several times over the next few years. I even took a group of friends on a Dartmoor jaunt that would become, for a while, an annual trip: we would arrive at Widecombe to scoff a cream tea, then march up and over the resplendent ridge of Hameldown, descending through ancient Grimspound, then on past the back of Headland Warren Farm, dropping down into the picture perfect valley beneath The Warren House Inn, and then finally up into the pub for pints, food and rest. That valley below the pub, in particular, has become a firm favourite spot, going on to earn the nickname *Paradise* amongst those in the know.

The yearning for that Devon landscape crept into my life in other ways too. My time in Bristol eventually came to an end as people began to drift away after university, with many of our group migrating to London to find work. Life in the big smoke held no allure for me though, it was the home turf of Devon that I craved, and eventually that's where I returned. I spent a great deal of time on the moor, visiting old haunts and new, and always making sure to end a good day's walking with a pint of fine ale and a packet of salty crisps.

The inevitable desire to successfully walk the Two Moors Way grew again slowly. On a visit to Devon for a fishing trip, a friend of mine made a remark about the lack of true wilderness in the UK. Initially I bristled against this vehemently – what about Dartmoor? Scotland? North Wales? I indignantly tried to prove him wrong, but over time I began to realise how right he was. His comment had riled me because it felt like a slight against Dartmoor, and therefore a slight against me and the treasured landscape of my youth, but in truth there are very few places you can go to in the UK that are truly isolated. Almost everywhere is within a few hours' walk of a town, or a village, a road, or at the very least some phone signal so you could be rescued in a pinch. By contrast, there are parts of North and South America, Africa, and Australia where you could find yourself hundreds of miles from the nearest sign of human civilisation, and if you were to find yourself there, your survival would be entirely down to your planning, your gear, your abilities, and nothing more.

This realisation stuck with me, and made me more determined than ever to seek out what wild landscapes I could. It also made me feel slightly foolish – if this moorland was so tame, so domestic, so manageable – then how did I spectacularly fail to conquer it twice in a row? Yes, I had drifted into that first attempt through an amiable enthusiasm and nothing more – but the second time I had been driven, and very much went into it with a desire to succeed. The common factor, it seemed, wasn't my inability to walk the distance but instead a lack of planning, or maybe a lack of engagement and commitment to the nature of the challenge itself. It's foolish to believe you can just throw on a pack and stumble hungover up a hill and assume you'll arrive at the end a few days later without a single hitch.

Thoughts like this made the stature of the route grow in my mind, and as my desire to attempt it again grew, so did the feeling that I needed to do it properly – to prepare, plan, train, and gear up in a way I'd never done before. As a result, I perpetually put it off. The time was never right, the weather was never perfect, I always had other things to do first.

Time moved on with it never becoming more than a lingering background thought. After a several years spent working away overseas, I returned to live in Devon once again with much of the angst of my twenties behind me. I moved into a little annexe flat with my partner, Siân, and I set up a small business in Exeter with another schoolfriend, Mark. One day, as Mark and I are sat at the desk in our office, he tells me that he's been looking at paying to sign up for a website that sets its members a series of challenges, in order to bring some adventure into his life. I am scathing of this idea, of course, like the eternal cynic I am – if he wants some challenges to make his life more adventurous, then I'll gladly set him some for free!

And so I do. I set him a series of challenges to be completed within the year, and with the completion of each one, I'll give him a little homemade badge. Within a month, he's enjoying the process so much that I relent and let him set me a series of challenges too.

Amongst the challenges I set him is the gauntlet laid down: walk the Two Moors Way. I partly set him this challenge because I think he'll enjoy it – he is more than capable, and it's a challenge fully worth undertaking – but I also do it for myself. I'm bringing the idea back out into the light, from unspoken ambition to a real event that's being actively discussed again, even if it's currently by someone else.

When Mark finally gets around to planning his walking challenge later in the year, I make sure he knows that I fully intend to join him.

THIRD ATTEMPT

'My frazzled state must be abundantly clear, as the lady behind the bar pauses and asks if maybe I wouldn't rather drink some water instead …'

AND SO – ONCE AGAIN – I step off the train at Ivybridge Station. It is a bright, clear August morning and the familiar rise of Butterdon Hill greets me like an old friend. I have new gear this time – no more *solar dry* trousers, they've long since been retired and sadly I never managed to find another pair for sale.* I have a new lightweight sleeping bag, solid walking boots, and a proper grown-up rucksack with a hydration pack tube snaking out of the top and down my shoulder strap. I have moisture wicking socks and a pair of shock absorbing walking poles. I am one of those people.

There are three of us undertaking the walk this time, yet I arrive at the station and set off walking alone. Both Mark and our mutual friend Dave have decided they want to do the Coast to Coast route – which is the Two Moors Way but with an added extension at the southern end that takes it all the way down to Wembury, on the South Devon coast. This is of little interest to me, as the goal of completing the Two Moors Way itself is too solid-ified in my mind to even consider changing or extending it. They assure me that they'll walk that first leg in the morning and meet me at Ivybridge at lunchtime so we can set off onto the moor together.

The three of us had met up about a week earlier to

---

* Clearly the world just wasn't ready for such a radical innovation.

discuss plans. It wasn't a very long conversation – officially it's Marks challenge, so he is calling most of the shots. I'm dubious about the timeframe they're talking about doing the walk in – not because I think four days is too few, but because they want to add on this extra leg at the start and still manage it in four days. In hindsight, I should've been way more concerned about that four day timeframe, but I misremembered the details of that second attempt: all I recalled was the four day trek we undertook, but memory is imperfect and tricksy – because of course we skipped out an entire day back then. In my eternal state of unpreparedness, I foolishly surmise that four days will be fine, and ultimately decide that if they want to add on an extra section at the start of the first day then it makes no odds to me – I will join them at Ivybridge and walk the opening section to Holne regardless, just as I've done twice before.

Standing at the station I can't get through to either of them on the phone, so I decide to set off up the hill on my own. I'd rather get the big climb done and then wait up on the moor, rather than here by the roadside. I pass the Dartmoor National Park Sign where I took those photographs all those years ago and feel a wave of nostalgia flood over me. Ten years have passed since I was last here. I thought I was a different person on that second attempt, only ten months after the first, but walking up to that sign after so much time has passed makes me feel at once deeply changed, and yet also entirely the same. I take a photo of it on my smartphone. As an act, it just doesn't feel as consequential.

Time has moved on, but the path up the hill remains unchanged. The golden sea of dry grass studded with a patchwork of red bracken and grey stone soars up towards the top of the ridge above, and I climb it steadily, stopping periodically to look behind at the world I am once again leaving behind. At the top of the rise, I stop and drop my pack. There are dark, shadowy clouds squatting offshore beyond the coastline, but they're a long way away and they don't seem like a threat to the soaring blue skies overhead. Eventually I manage to get through to Dave – they've been a bit delayed but they're about an hour away from where I am. I'm itching to get walking and put some distance between myself and the start line, so sitting there waiting for an hour isn't all that appealing, no matter how beautiful the view is. I tell them I'll keep walking on, but slowly so they can catch me up. I shoulder my pack again and set off.

Walking at this pace allows me to take in this stretch of the southern moor in far greater detail. I veer off the path and scramble up to the rocky peak of Butterdon Hill for the first time, flitting amongst the huge granite boulders and taking a moment to scale to the very top of the tor, a fractured heap of rock that juts up above the hilltop. It provides a perfect promontory from which to survey the entire world.

I continue at a slow but steady pace along the ridge as it heads north. To my left is the steep sided valley that holds the winding River Erme, to my right is the thin stretch of woodland that runs along the length of the Avon as it flows out of the reservoir and down towards the town of South Brent. At the point where the path forks, I stop and wait again, laying my pack on the ground and resting my head against it with my back on the cool grass. It's the hottest part of the day, and whilst it feels strange to be dawdling so intentionally, it's also making this whole thing feel like a breeze. It gives me a great deal of confidence that this time I might just make it to the end.

After a quick nap in the sun, I drink some water and decide to move on. If they were only an hour behind me then they must be getting close now. I resume at the same slow and steady pace along the path towards the strange quarry site that Sam and I stopped by for lunch at all those years ago. I dawdle and linger there, now slightly concerned that I still haven't been joined by my walking companions. I call them again – it turns out Mark has developed blisters where his boots have been rubbing, but his feet are now all dressed and they're back on their way. The sun is still high in the sky, but it's now about 3pm and I know how much further there is to go from here. I decide not to linger, but instead just to get going.

Mark is a unique character. I've known him since we were teenagers, and in that time he's been a scruffy punk, a weekend reenactment buff, a besuited 1930s gentleman, and a kilt wearing weightlifter – amongst a variety of other iterations. He has a tendency to discover his latest aesthetic passion and immerse himself in it completely – and for this walk he hasn't disappointed, kitting himself out with vintage leather army boots, a canvas pack complete with an old iron frame, woollen kilt and knee-high socks, a newsboy cap, a stout wooden walking stick, and an array of classic vintage hiking gear. He looks like he's stepped out of a hiking journal from 1923 (and also a little bit like an overgrown *Just William*), but the fact that he's gotten himself blisters so early on isn't really all that surprising. Dave is more no-nonsense about things, instead of dressing up for the occasion he will likely be far more concerned with maximising his walking speed and covering ground as fast as possible. Despite their differing priorities, both are more athletic than I am by nature, and I have no doubt they'll be moving at a much faster pace than I can, no matter whether I linger or not.

An hour later I'm standing at the top of the Avon River valley, looking down at the crossing, and away toward the tussocky ground up the side of the Hill From Hell that's caught me out on both previous occasions. From here, taking the time to actually stop and survey the land ahead, I can clearly see where we went wrong: the path does a feint through the marsh and then eventually disappears somewhere in the long grass, but now I can also see a smaller, less enticing track that flits between the reeds nearer the river bank and hops a section of fence, before skirting the near side of the marsh and then sweeping up to the top of the hill round to the east – tussock free and plain sailing. From this vantage I can see what an easy mistake it is to make – if you haven't checked the route in advance, that is.

Before descending I look behind to see if the figures of Mark and Dave have appeared on the horizon. At this point I'm secretly hoping that they haven't – I've now picked up my pace and I'm trying to see if I can beat them to Holne, even with my slower gait. Plus I'm enjoying spending this time in the beautiful moorland with nothing but my pack and my own thoughts.

I stop at the river and take off my shoes and socks. The day is hot but the water is cool, and it feels great letting my feet soak for a bit. Now that I've stopped idling so much I am beginning to notice how unfit I've become. I am only halfway through the first day of the walk – most of which I've taken at a very leisurely pace – but already the straps are dragging on my shoulders, my legs are tired, and my feet are sore. I have become distinctly doughy as time has slipped by, and whilst I do still walk and cycle plenty, I don't tend to do it with the same sense of purpose and gusto that I once did.

After all this time, I still have the route of the first two days of the walk pretty firmly etched into my memory, and so I sit by the river for a while and go through the remainder of the day in my head. All I need to do is successfully make my way up the Hill From Hell, then it's a swift cruise over the crest and down to the tree line at Chalk Ford, before a simple scurry down the lane to Scorriton. I can wait in the pub there for the guys to catch me up, and we can do the last stretch to Holne together. I gaze down the valley towards the reservoir in the distance, seeing the point where the river billows out wide into a calm, flat pool. With the sun drifting over the hilltops behind, it casts the scene in a haze of orange and pink. I may be flagging, but it still feels really good to be back on the path.

Thirty minutes later, I am frothing with fury as I find myself waist deep in tussocks once again. How is this even possible? I've picked my route so carefully, and yet still found myself staggering through hideous hidden crevices that alternate with ankle-snappingly shallow thickets of dense grass. I try to steer myself back to the east where I know the path lies, but there's something about this hill that gets me all turned around, and the fragmented ground seems to extend infinitely in every direction. I am so annoyed that I just stamp forwards at full pelt, not caring if I injure myself – I just want to find the path again. It's not fair.

Miraculously I don't injure myself, but I do arrive at the top of the hill completely out of puff. I drink some water and chomp down an energy bar, but the desire to stop and have a long sit down is getting pretty overwhelming. This does not bode well for the rest of the trip.

Looking over my shoulder towards the other side of the valley, I'm fairly sure I can make out the shapes of two figures descending toward the river. This is enough motivation for me to set off again as I've now decided that I want to be in the pub when they arrive, looking all smug at having reached there so long before they did. This would be entirely unwarranted of course – they will have walked twice the distance I have – but the idea of them catching me now seems like it would be a let-down, and so I quickly march on. The gorse studded slope down to Chalk Ford is far longer than it is in my memory, and by the time I get to the little wooden bridge that crosses the twisting stream into the woods, it is almost dark and I am very, very tired.

The climb back up from the stream on the far side is long and arduous. Or at least it feels it – I'm sure it was shorter before. At the top of the rise where the track meets the narrow lane into Scorriton, I meet an elderly farming couple, standing next to their Land Rover. They've mislaid some sheep out on the moor, but it's too dark to search now so they're heading back to the village, asking if I'd like a lift. In a moment of ridiculous and misplaced honesty, I decline. I'm walking the Two Moors Way, I say, driving is cheating. About thirty seconds after their vehicle disappears from view and I start creakily walking again, it occurs to me that this was a huge mistake. Why did I say that? I could've been in the pub by now, and instead I still have over a mile of rocky track to stumble down in the ever-growing darkness.

On the bright side though, before they set off they offer me use of a fallow field of theirs to use as a campsite for the night. This is very kind of them, and I take a mental note of its location: an unlocked gate opposite a lone oak tree, not far from the village. I keep on marching down the track, now in full darkness and aching all over. I consider just how desperately out of shape I am, and I how much I need my reward of a pint and some crisps to make it all ok.

The Tradesman's Arms in Scorriton is as honest a pub as you could hope for, full of friendly staff, good beer and a cosy atmosphere. I stagger inside and fling my sweat-soaked pack against the bar, immediately ordering a well-earned pint. My frazzled state must be abundantly clear, as the lady behind the bar pauses and asks if maybe I wouldn't rather drink some water instead. That's not the kind of sensible advice I'm looking for – I need beer and crisps! But yes also some water would be good too, thankyouverymuch. I drink about half the pint in one go and I'm just attempting to manoeuvre my aching torso onto a bar stool when the pub door opens behind me and in walk Mark and Dave. There isn't really any way I can try and pull off the old "what kept you I've been here for ages" routine, and besides, they both look exactly how I feel.

They order their own pints and we head to the bench outside to drop all our baggage and sit down. All three of us are thirsty, sore, and absolutely exhausted. I fail to raise the fact that they've walked twice as far as me today and that I'm mostly in this state because of how unfit I am, and instead get involved with the shared complaining – swapping tales of blisters, hateful tussocks, and comparing just how heavy our packs are.

It's pretty clear none of us have any intention of carrying on to Holne this evening, and so I tell them about the friendly farmers and their offer of a field to camp in – just a little way back up the path we came down, an unlocked gate opposite a solitary oak tree. We shoulder our rucksacks again with some difficulty and begin walking back the way we came. In the fifteen minutes since we sat down, our bodies have clearly all decided we've done enough walking for one day and have promptly seized up. We stagger back uphill in the dark looking for an unlocked gate opposite a solitary oak tree. We find several. There are many gates lining the track, and it turns out a great deal of them have oak trees standing opposite them. We flounder in the dark for a while, before eventually picking one of the unlocked gates at random and hoping for the best. If someone wants us to leave their field, they can come and tell us. Otherwise we're making camp and falling asleep.

We stretch out a canvas sheet between the trees and lay our bedding beneath it. Dave produces a metal fire pit from inside his rucksack and gets a small blaze going. Mark opens his pack and brings out a glass jar of Dolmio sauce, along with some pasta, and a small cheese board. I am no longer sure whether the reason they are so exhausted is because they've walked 30 miles, or because they've packed enough equipment and luxury food to feed a small army. Probably both. I think back on Sam and I living off lukewarm rice and pesto spoonfuls, crammed inside his one man tent.

We sit by the fire inspecting our sore feet and warming our aching limbs. We don't like our prospects for making the whole trip right now, given how today went. I am a tad embarrassed by my clear physical decline, and Mark is most likely regretting his choices of rations and antique gear – not that he'd ever admit as much out loud. It's at this point that the foolishness of thinking we can do it all in four days really dawns on me. I start to think back over those previous attempts and it's only then that I remember the bus ride out of Widecombe to Exeter and on to Morchard Bishop, cutting a whole day out of the route. I decide it's probably better not to mention it. Captain Hindsight is rarely a welcome contributor.

Whilst striking camp in the morning, Dave declares he's going to call his wife and get a lift home. He'd rather cut his losses and try again another time, better prepared. Mark and I decide to press on; perhaps if we can leave some of our excess gear with Dave then we can travel a bit lighter and make better time. We set off all together, as Dave is getting picked up from Newbridge car park. We're all still feeling the strain after yesterday's assault on our bodies, but it's a fresh morning and the lanes to Holne are fairly easy going. The Church House Inn is still closed this early, but we knock on the door anyway to see if someone will be willing to fill our water bottles. A friendly lady answers, obliges and sends us on our way; we begin the descent down the Dart Valley, greedily drinking our days' water supply immediately.

The path that follows the rushing river down the valley is reinvigorating, and arriving at the peaceful meander that wraps around the green plateau at Spitchwick just as the sun begins to warm the ground is delightful. We need to wait here for Dave's lift to arrive, so we strip down to our underwear and throw ourselves in the river. The channel here is perfect for swimming; the water is clear and the current slow moving. After our dip we lay out on the warm grass and eat some breakfast while we wait, taking the downtime to try and restore as much energy as we can for the walk ahead.

Before Dave leaves, Mark and I go through our bags and discard some of our unnecessary equipment for him to take away, then we shoulder our slightly lighter loads and get moving. The next section is the long haul up Newbridge Hill and then along Dr Blackall's Drive all the way up to Bel Tor, and I know from past experience that it's a long, slow climb. By the time I've propelled myself halfway up the ridge, I'm already feeling the grind again. We take as many breaks as we can manage, but the day is getting hot and it's a sweaty, relentless ascent. Once at the top we don't waste any more time with breaks as time is pressing on, instead heading straight back down the other side of the ridge towards Ponsworthy. It's almost midday by the time we arrive at the spring there, where we refill our bottles again. The heat beating down is sapping what little strength I have remaining.

Once again, the decision to take a detour via Widecombe seems the sensible course of action. Walking the lanes toward the village seems to make our swollen feet more painful than ever, and when we finally arrive in the village and deposit ourselves into a café for a cream tea it seems like sweet relief. As we eat quietly, it doesn't take long for us to come to the mutual consensus that we're not going to carry on any further. Even if we could drag ourselves onward and get to Chagford by this evening, there's no way we'll be in any state to make it all the way to Lynmouth this time around.

We finish eating and use the last of our energy to walk a little way out of the village to the Rugglestone Inn, so we can drink some pints whilst we await rescue. The

Rugglestone is a strange little pub, with barely enough room to fit two people shoulder-to-shoulder in the bar area, but a large, open beer garden outside full of exotic ducks and chickens. The sun is out and it warms my back as we let the weight lift from our tired feet. After a while, our friend Rupert rocks up to take us back to reality in his car, but instead of jumping in and heading off home, we drink more beers together amongst the weird chickens and tell him of our misadventures. He ends up sticking about for dinner in the pub and the three of us camp out on the grass opposite, just for one extra night under the stars.

Strangely, unlike before, I don't feel all that deflated this time. My attitude towards the challenge has changed it seems. I see this less as a failure and more as simply another lesson in bad planning decisions – it's very clear exactly what can be learned from this and what I could do differently next time. The key thing is that the idea is now out of the recesses of my mind and back into the realm of reality once again; I know it won't be long until I'm back out here. Maybe next time with the right gear, the right schedule, the right supplies – maybe next time will be the time I finally manage to find the magic combination that gets me to the end at last.

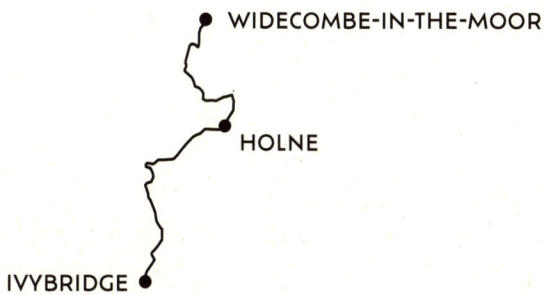

WIDECOMBE-IN-THE-MOOR

HOLNE

IVYBRIDGE

FOURTH ATTEMPT

SUMMER

*'Mid Devon stretches onward over stile, stream,
and hill indefinitely'*

THE SHADOWS ARE STARTING TO grow long as I make the descent from the top of the hill that leads down towards Chalk Ford. This is now the fourth time I've picked my way through this honeycomb maze of diverging paths that wind through the gorse thickets and scrub to the bottom of the hill, but it's the first time I've ever made it here in time to see daylight reveal the bubbling, twisting brook rushing underneath the old wooden bridge. I set out from Ivybridge Station earlier this morning on my first ever entirely solo attempt. I know the route of this first day like the back of my hand now, and I smash through it with relative ease – even finally managing to avoid the tussock-induced madness of the Hill From Hell – instead actually finding the real path that skirts the marsh and takes me up to the top with glorious ease. It seems so obvious now I've actually studied the map in advance. I'm on track to make it to Scorriton by 6pm, where I intend to grab a beer and then take a leisurely stroll up to Holne for some food in the Church House Inn. So far, it's all going swimmingly.

It had been almost exactly a year since the third attempt. Mark and I had both managed to finish our respective sets of challenges – with the exception of his Two Moors Way challenge of course – and with the advent of the new year we decided to do it all again. There were more people involved this time, a group of about ten friends setting up a year's worth of personal challenges for each other. The Two Moors Way challenge was – inevitably – set for Mark, Dave, and myself this time: by the end of the year, we each had to have completed it.

We talked for a while about trying it as a trio together again, but Dave had developed some crazy notion about doing the whole thing in just two days, so Mark and I quickly wrote ourselves out of that wild plan and tried to see if we could manage to do it with just the two of us. As the year rolled on, it became clear that organising a time where we could both take a week away from work together was almost impossible. Come June, Mark undertook the walk on his own, with a more sensible array of equipment, and less glass jars of pasta sauce and decadent cheeseboards. He made it to Lynmouth over the course of six easy-going days without any major incidents.*

A month or so later, Dave made his attempt. He roped in Eve, his wife, to try and do the entire thing in two days – they made it all the way to Drewsteignton on the northern edge of Dartmoor in fifteen straight hours, before Eve dropped out and Dave completed the remainder of the route on his own over two more brutal days of

---

* Which I found inspiring and infuriating in equal measure.

relentless pace. I enjoy the process of walking and taking in my surroundings far too much to ever even consider smashing through it like that in such an intense fashion, but it's impossible to deny that his three day assault on the moors was anything but insanely impressive.

With Mark and Dave having each finished the route in time to complete their challenges, it was now just up to me to finally achieve what I started thirteen years ago. With the months rapidly whizzing by and the challenge deadline quickly approaching, I secured a week off work at the end of August and began to prepare.

A few weeks before I set off, however, the ever-changing needs of running a business had bulldozed their way into my best laid plans, meaning I had to reduce my booked time off to just half a week. Not a problem, I thought – I can just complete the walk in two stages and still have completed the entire thing by the end of the year. It's not how I'd always envisioned it, but maybe it would actually help to do it that way. I looked ahead and found a three day weekend in early October I could take for the second half.

The new plan was to get from Ivybridge to Holne on day one, then to Chagford on day two, and Morchard Bishop on day three, before being picked up by Siân, and driven home ready to work again the next day. I'd then resume from Morchard Bishop in October, stopping at Knowstone and Simonsbath overnight, before arriving in Lynmouth at the end of the weekend.

After a quick break for a pint, I leave the Tradesman's Arms in Scorriton and head towards Holne – my stopping point for the night. The road dips down into the valley below then crosses a little stone bridge over the river before climbing up once again toward the village. The day has been hot, but the trickle of water under the bridge adds to the touch of cool in the evening air, and I feel in surprisingly good shape. I'm a little fitter than I was this time last year – still not exactly at my physical peak, but I have enough training walks under my belt to aid my confidence. One of my many challenges the previous year was to cycle to Bristol, over 100 miles of navigating winding lanes and sweat-soaked hills, and the process of preparing for and undertaking that journey has set me in good stead. I've also lightened the load in my rucksack: this time I have a hydration pack, a few items of clothing, a lightweight sleeping bag and pillow, a waterproof bivvy bag, and some snack bars. My plan is to travel light, eat at pubs and cafes, and sleep in my bivvy to avoid carrying a tent.

I make my way along the lanes towards Holne at a gentle pace, feeling confident in having made good time and not wanting to push myself too far on day one. I reach The Church House Inn as the sun is starting to give way to the night, and order a sandwich, some chips and a pint to a table outside so I can eat and drink as I watch the stars come out. It's incredibly peaceful.

After leaving the Church House Inn, I head up the hill out of the village and hop the stile to find the field where Sam and I camped on those first two attempts. Unfortunately, it's been cordoned off with an electric fence and filled with grazing sheep, only leaving the bridle path running down the left-hand side and not allowing for any wild camping. Disappointed, I continue down the path and through a gate that allows me into the next field, further down the valley. This one is still open and potentially good for a camping spot, but there are couple of horses grazing and I think better about sleeping in the grass with them loose nearby. I continue downward again into the final field before the path heads back into the treeline below. It is empty, but the grass is long and unkempt – not ideal for camping. I follow the hedge along the top edge to try and find a slightly clearer spot where I can set up my bedroll. There's an area beneath the base of an old apple tree that seems a bit earthier and less grassy. I stamp the offending undergrowth flat and then lay out my bivvy bag, pushing my sleeping bag into it, along with a lightweight inflatable ground mat, then climb inside. The tiny inflatable pillow I've got is pretty worthless, but I push it into the hood of my sleeping bag anyway, just so there's something under my head. It's not particularly comfortable, but being able to sleep under a clear night sky with the stars above is enough of a spell-binding experience that it doesn't really matter. I drift off to sleep feeling very pleased with my first day's progress.

About an hour later I am jolted awake by the sensation of something cold and wet against my neck. I lurch upright in my sleeping bag, and the enveloping bivvy follows me, hauling the stiff ground mat along with it and catapulting my tiny pillow off into the night. I don't care about that though; I'm just trying to free my arms from their downy straitjacket so I can flick away whatever is on my neck. After a struggle with the internal zip, I free an arm and swing it around to fling away a slug that's clambered into my sleeping bag and plopped itself onto my neck. I retch with disgust.

Reaching over to grab the headtorch from my pack, I flick it on to see the true horror that surrounds me. From out of the knee-high grass, an army of slithering creatures have appeared. They're all over my bivvy, my sleeping bag and a few have managed to make it inside. I shoot out of the bag and grab a nearby stick to flick them away with. I am now standing in the middle of the field in my underpants – headtorch strapped on, stick in hand – frantically beating back the onslaught of slugs like a madman.

It takes a while to ascertain that both my sleeping bag and bivvy are slug free. I retrieve my (now very damp) pillow from across the field and clamber back inside to get warm. In the darkness all around me I feel I can hear the slithering and creeping of a thousand slugs that seem to be inexorably drawn to me. Eventually I prop my bedroll up against the loose mass of my rucksack to give myself some clearance from the ground, and I put my headtorch back on so I can see if any of them get too close. I spend the whole night like this – periodically nodding off and then suddenly lurching awake again to beat away the onslaught of slimy marauders.

First light creeps over the horizon, tentatively lifting the hood of the night sky and softly breathing its warm glow through the treeline. I am lying in a field, wrapped in multiple layers of dew-damp sleeping gear, propped up against a half empty bag with a torch strapped to my head and clutching a stick. I must look like the only survivor of an overnight zombie attack. That's more or less how I feel.

As soon as it's light enough to see, I give up pretending to sleep and stuff my damp belongings into my pack. I clumsily tie my boots and set off down the hill, just wanting to be anywhere but the scene of gastropod horror. Stumbling down the Dart Valley, I am not at all taking in the majestic grandeur of the water or any of that waffle, I'm just staggering onwards in the hope I'll be able to find somewhere that I might still be able to get a few hours' undisturbed sleep now that it's daylight. Eventually I make it to Spitchwick once again. The sun is warming the ground now and the quieter stretch of babbling river is calming, so I lay out my damp sleeping gear in the sun to dry out, and sit down on a rock next to the water. Within seconds I am fast asleep.

It never takes long for a spot as accessible and beautiful as Spitchwick to fill with visitors. I've probably only been asleep an hour when I get rudely awoken by a rogue dog pelting towards me in hot pursuit of an idly thrown stick. There are families setting up for the day and adventurers getting ready to take to the water. Most people don't seem to be paying me any mind, but I do get a few strange looks from those who think it's weird that I'm fast asleep on the floor with my possessions strewn around me. I wearily repack my bag, eat some snack bars and drink some water. All of the momentum I was feeling from yesterday's successful walk is now gone.

The following climb up Newbridge Hill and along the ridge towards Bel Tor is tough going. Walking alone is a very different experience – you get the advantage of setting your own pace, stopping whenever you want, and making all your own decisions, but at the same time you have no one to push you onwards when you're flagging, or help you through the tough sections with distracting chatter. I stop regularly for short breaks just to get some energy back. The sun on my face and the light breeze up on the exposed hillside is refreshing at first, but I am still low on energy after so little sleep and in the heat I'm starting to feel that unpleasant itchy stickiness that comes from being exhausted and hungry and dirty and sweaty all at once.

A yawning funnel of trees guides me from the open moor into the shelter of the next valley as the winding path meets the lane that drops down towards Ponsworthy. The descent is steep but lush with overhanging greenery that provides shelter from the elements, in a direct contrast to the long, open ridge I've just left behind. I take a break in the shade of the hamlet, filling up my water bottle at the spring and sitting by the water a while. As with every attempt, I've decided to a take a detour to Widecombe for lunch. It would seem rude not to really. The two and a half mile walk down the lanes towards Widecombe has been a bit of a trudge every time, as it's always strange to leave the scenic pathways of the route to instead follow the restrictive hedge-lined lanes for such a prolonged period, but it's ultimately worth it to eventually stop into The Old Inn and drop my pack on the floor inside. I order some food and find a shady spot in the garden to try and recuperate for the afternoon's walking. The next stretch over Hameldown is one I know very well – it seems strange that this will only be the second time I've actually walked it as part a Two Moors Way attempt.

I may be feeling tired from the slug-induced lack of sleep, but I've got plenty of time to make it to Chagford before nightfall. I've also got the reward of a stop-off at the Warren House Inn to look forward to, so I decide to set off without delay, so I can be sure to pace myself. If I can just drag my flagging body to the end of the day's walk then I can get a proper night's sleep and be ready to tackle a whole new section of the route tomorrow. The biggest mistake I could make now is to push too hard and injure myself.

Picking my way over loose stones and the bare dirt of a long since dried up stream bed, I climb steadily up the flank of Hameldown and enjoy the slow ascent to greet the view at the glorious peak. It's a huge help to know these long sections of the route so well: I can envisage them in my mind's eye, partition them up and meter out my energy as needed. I linger a while at Hameldown Beacon, soaking in the scenery. Dartmoor extends in all directions, shimmering in a summer heat-haze, the crystal blue of the sky descending into the blurry brown and green of the sun-baked earth. No matter how exhausted I am, I will never tire of such spectacle.

I drop down through Grimspound and follow the rough track around Headland Warren Farm and onward to Paradise – the beautiful little valley where the path crosses a gently flowing stream beneath an old oak tree. Tucked behind it are the ruins of an old stone building – just a couple of walls remain crumbling into the surrounding grass, but it's enough to add to the air of ancient tranquillity that permeates the scene. It's hard not to linger here, and I consider grabbing dinner in the Warren House and then heading back down here to camp for the night, but I know it would take me too far off schedule. I climb back out of the valley and on towards to the welcome embrace of the inn.

I pick up my well-earned pint and crisps and head

back outside to enjoy the view as I reward myself. I haven't reached Chagford yet, but it's only couple of miles over the common – provided I can avoid spraining my knee again. Outside, I'm joined by Rupert and couple of other friends; they're keen to share a beer with me and check in on my journey. It's a little strange to have people from the real world re-enter my consciousness after two days alone on the moor, but their company is uplifting and welcome. It doesn't take long to convince me to stay for another pint, and then to head inside for some food with them. By the time we're wrapping it up I look outside to realise the sun has set and the stars are out. I'm wary of walking over the common in the dark, particularly after spraining my knee in this exact spot on the first attempt, so I eventually accept a lift, thinking to myself that it's only a mile or two that I'll be skipping.

After spending longer in the car than I'd expected, Rupert drops me off on the outskirts of Chagford and I begin walking in the dark towards the town, keeping an eye out for a good spot to set up for the night. I feel a little guilty for hitching a lift, but the lingering tiredness I've been staving off all day has now entirely floored me, and I tell myself it would've been dangerous to go wandering off onto the moor during the night in this state. I follow a track up to the playing field just south of the town and clamber up the bank that takes me onto the smooth, grassy sports pitch. It seems strange to sleep on a playing field, but at the same time I am haunted by the memory of the slug attack the night before and the idea of setting up my bedroll on an expanse of clear, perfectly clipped grass is very appealing.* I spend the first hour or so cautiously clutching my head-torch and shining it at anything that moves across the grass in the darkness, but the feared gastropod attack never emerges, and eventually tiredness overtakes me and I fall into a deep sleep.

There are few settlements on Dartmoor, and most of those are tiny, perfectly preserved hamlets and villages with beautiful thatched cottages and babbling streams running through them. Chagford, on the other hand, is a bit of an anomaly – along with nearby Moretonhampstead, it actually exists as a relatively modern and flourishing town. It contains a school, a small supermarket, a variety of art galleries, and a spectacular hardware shop that seems to have been imported from the world of Harry Potter – so full of twisting wooden stairwells and impossible geometry that it's easy to get lost in for hours. My dad still goes there every year to do his Christmas shopping, buying Ordnance Survey maps from the section next to the rat poison, or grabbing Wellington boots from the cupboard behind the sledgehammers.

Given that Chagford is livelier and more bustling

* Relatively speaking, of course …

than most of the places I've stayed, it's hardly surprising when the sound of nearby voices wakes me with a start. It's already fully daylight, I'm very wet and I've got a serious crick in my neck. Thankfully though, unlike the night before, I have actually managed to sleep. Blearily looking around, I notice some movement outside the small building on the far side of the playing field. After a minute, it becomes clear that there's a crowd of kids gathering, and they're most likely gearing up for a game of football on this fine morning – it is a Saturday after all. Wild campers aren't an unusual sight on the open moor, but a strange man sleeping in a damp bag on a kid's playing field is a suspicious sight anywhere. I haul myself out of my soggy bed as quickly and quietly as possible and slip away into the trees below the pitch.

I grab a coffee and some pastries from a bakery in the little village centre then head north along the road to rejoin the trail as it dances alongside the River Teign. I've slept but I don't feel particularly refreshed, so I'm relying on coffee and sugar to kickstart my body and trick it into walking for another full day. It's gloriously sunny again though, and following the winding river through the fields is spectacular. The path chases the flowing water into the woods before reappearing again at Mill End and then snaking off up the side of the Teign Gorge. This whole stretch is almost too beautiful; the river sparkles and the hills swoop and the perfectly green trees line the steep sides of the gorge with an almost sponge-like texture. It feels like walking in Middle Earth.

It takes me a while to ascend the steep track up the gorge's side, and at the top I nearly keel over now that the day is reaching full heat. I rest on a bench to cool off and look out over the glorious view that stretches away into oblivion. I'm soon joined by another walker and we strike up a brief conversation. It turns out he is also walking the Two Moors Way, although he's heading from Lynmouth southwards towards Ivybridge.* He's a muscular chap with a resolute expression, and he has an efficient looking pack on his back. I wonder if he's perhaps ex-military. Either way, he clearly isn't finding this whole thing as difficult as I am, so I fail to mention that this is in fact my fourth attempt. As we part ways and I continue northward, it occurs to me for the first time that I'm now walking a section of the route I've never been on before.

I arrive in the tiny village of Drewsteignton at about 11am. The pub isn't open until 12, but I decide to wait around so I can grab some lunch. Beyond here the route leaves Dartmoor and heads out into mid Devon, where shops and pubs are sparser, and it will likely be a good few hours before I come across somewhere else I can get food. I set myself up on a bench outside the churchyard to pass the time. After about five minutes it starts to gently rain. I continue to sit awhile anyway as

* Common sense dictates that north to south is downhill, and therefore easier.

the cooling air and the smell of petrichor is a pleasant change. After a few minutes more, it starts to absolutely pelt it down – I'm now scrambling to dig my waterproofs out of my bag as I scurry to find shelter. I hide in an overgrown bus-stop until it eases off and I emerge again, now sweating inside my waterproof and soaked by the English summer rain. I get myself into the pub as soon as it opens, order a sandwich and get my wet things laid out on a bench to dry.

North of Drewsteignton the trail leads over the concrete rush of the A30 and leaves the moor behind, the landscape becoming less craggy, ancient beauty and more rustic charm. I enter the first of many farmers' fields, sticking to the edge in order to keep my footprint on their land as minimal as possible. There is a large herd of cows at the bottom of the field; I wave at them as I draw near. They seem strangely interested in me – cows are normally quite happy to mind their own business, but as I approach they all begin to turn round and trot towards me. This is a strange turn of affairs – I am not worried by cows as a rule, but they're big creatures with a lot of momentum and when there's a herd of them moving in your direction it's best to get out of the way. I step up my pace towards the gate at the far end of the hedgerow I'm following. As I step up my pace, so do they. Increasingly rattled, I break into a run. So do they. I am now running towards the gate with a herd of about thirty cows bearing down on me.

Realising they're gaining on me, my brain clicks into self-preservation mode and instead of trying to reach the gate, my body decides to fling itself over the barbed wire fence that bounds the hedgerow beside me. I clear it in one leap and collapse heavily into the knot of branches and tree roots beyond. Heaving myself up, I scrabble through the hedge and into the field on the other side. This is clearly not a field that I'm meant to be in, and in the near distance I'm pretty sure I can make out some huge tractor or farm machine going about its business. I creep back along the hedge in the direction I came from until I reach a collapsing old gate wrapped up in barbed wire. Peering over I can see the herd of cows in the other field, now standing confused at the spot where I vanished into the undergrowth. After some consideration, I try to carefully climb the gate so that I can re-enter the field quietly, then circle around the far side, giving the cows a wide berth to make it to the stile that will lead me out and on my way. As I try to balance myself unsteadily on the lower bar, I catch my arm on the barbed wire, letting out a yelp and wobbling precariously. I steady myself on the gate and look up to see the herd now ponderously heading over toward me, seeming quite perplexed. Within a minute they're surrounding the gap on the other side of the gate. They're not going to make this easy for me.

Behind, I can hear the sound of the distant tractor drawing closer. I'm sure any reasonable farmer would just laugh at my strange predicament, but I'd still rather not wait around to find out. I decide to sneak back down this side of the hedge towards the far end of the field where the exit stile stands, then make a break, through the hedge, over the barbed wire, and across the stile as quickly as I can, hoping I can make it before the herd notices and catches me. I execute my plan almost entirely imperfectly, getting my rucksack snagged in the hedge, collapsing into a cow pat as I stack it over the fence, and then scrambling to make it to the stile as the herd bear down on me. After my heart-stopping bovine brush with death, I stagger a short way into the field beyond and drop my bag, feeling very shaken and surprised to be attacked by a group of placid herbivores. It's only later that it dawns on me that they're likely being drawn to the sound of my tin cup clanging on the side of my bag. I'd wager good money that the farmer clangs some kind of bell or steel bowl when they bring the day's feed out for the cattle.

Mid Devon stretches onward over stile, stream, and hill indefinitely; moving through farmyards, skirting fields full of crops, and weaving around the backs of isolated cottage gardens each in full bloom. It's like being in a Beatrix Potter story, as opposed to the Tolkienesque wilds of Dartmoor. Eventually I reach Hittisleigh, a tiny village whose main feature seems to be a crossroads with a bench. I sit at the bench for a while, now eight miles into an eighteen mile day, and as my shoulders sag it occurs to me that in my current state, making it to Morchard Bishop today is almost definitely going to be too much for me. I am tired and sore and aching all over, covered in barbed wire scratches and a sticky patina of old sweat. I find a phone box and dig out some pennies in order to call Siân, who is supposed to be collecting me from the end point this evening. We both study the map to try and figure out somewhere on the remaining route that she might be able to find me in a few hours so that I can keep walking for now, and hopefully cover some more ground with what remains of my energy. After a while, it becomes clear that there isn't anywhere obvious that will work, given how off the beaten path the route is. I either need to be picked up from Hittisleigh, or commit to making it all the way to Morchard Bishop. After brief consideration, I decide to call it here.

I head back over to the bench by the crossroads to await my lift home. It really is a very nice bench.

AUTUMN

'For a minute I just stand there and stare at my own legs, contemplating the point where they disappear beneath the surface ...'

IT's BRIGHT AND EARLY WHEN I arrive back at the crossroads in Hittisleigh after a five week interval. There's still some residual warmth in the air, but the days are notably shorter now and the clouds are hurrying through the sky above, morphing as they roll along in ever changing shades of grey and white. I pick up right where I left off and head onward, away from the bench, more determined than ever to cover ground and see this attempt through to the end.

I hadn't felt all that bad about stopping early on that third day in August. It would've been nice to make it to Morchard Bishop by the evening and to have been on track with the plan I'd originally laid out, but at the same time I felt pretty proud of myself: that was the longest unbroken stint of walking the Two Moors Way I'd ever done, making it entirely across Dartmoor and out into mid Devon for the first time. I'd already accepted that I'd be doing this in two sections whether I liked it or not – so it wasn't over yet. I also felt fairly confident that the problem had been the lack of sleep, and I was sure that if I'd managed to rest properly at the end of each day, I would've had far more energy and would've made it to the end, rather than slowly fading away as the days dragged on.

I did, however, now have to ready myself for the next phase. I didn't have the time to add on another day, and so I would need to absorb the missed ten mile section – from Hittisleigh to Morchard Bishop – into the first day's walk, extending it to well over twenty six miles. If I'd learned anything from my previous misadventures, it was that this wasn't something I was capable of doing.

So instead my new plan was to walk to Witheridge on the first day, instead of Knowstone – a much more manageable sixteen miles. Then I would pass through Knowstone on the way to Simonsbath the day after – a much longer twenty one miles – then followed by a short, final eleven mile day to see me all the way to Lynmouth, and the long awaited completion of the walk. To make things easier, I decided to abandon camping entirely and just stay in pubs on the route. No more sleeping in damp, slug infested sacks for me; I was going to do this in *style*. I booked a room in the Mitre Inn in Witheridge for the Friday night, and then the Forest Inn in Simonsbath for Saturday. The plan was for Siân to meet me at the Forest Inn that evening, and then to drive to Lynmouth as I set off the next morning in order to meet me at the end. It was going to be a long weekend of walking, but this was easily the most planning I'd ever put into making it all work – and it had to work, because I knew I had to finish the route by the end of the year, and the year was rapidly coming to a close.

After setting off from the crossroads, I spend the first hour or two ambling down quiet country lanes as they zig-zag back and forth along the contours of undulating valleys. Eventually the route veers north, away from the road, and dives back into the roughly hewn tracks that skim the edges of farm fields, scramble through dotted copses, and shamble down ancient holloways. At one point the path gives way to an old disused railway line that cleaves the countryside in two from east to west within a perfectly train-sized tunnel of overhanging trees. Standing in the middle of the tracks and seeing the endless straight metal disappearing off into the distance both directions is a disorienting sensation.

After several hours of winding my way through this landscape, I come within a stone's throw of the small village of Morchard Road. I can see on the map that it would be a relatively minor detour to make my way there and find some lunch, but instead I decide to hold fast to the trail and stick it out to Morchard Bishop a few miles further on. If I stop there for lunch instead then I'll be over half way to Witheridge, meaning I'll have broken the back of today's walk before taking my first proper rest, allowing me to ease off during the afternoon and take a gentler pace.

Another hour of rolling through fields and hills at last brings me into Morchard Bishop. I stop at the same little shop where George, Sam, and I had picked up the route ten years earlier, grabbing myself some sandwiches and snacks to fuel my journey. As I stand outside eating, I notice the dark clouds starting to appear beyond the hill behind me, bringing the threat of rain to the afternoon's walk. About an hour later, on approach to Black Dog – the last village before reaching Witheridge – the threat is made real and the heavens open in an awesome deluge. My waterproofs are helpless against this onslaught, and I dive beneath a broad oak tree to find any kind of shelter for a while. The sky turns dark grey and the rain comes down with jabbing sideways flurries that somehow manage to get under my hood. I eventually reason that this isn't going anywhere and it's time to just press on and accept the thorough soaking.

Trudging through field after field in the rain as the mud begins to splatter up my shins isn't much fun. At a point where the path briefly crosses the road, I instead decide to change course and follow the tarmac into Black Dog rather than stay offroad. I make quicker progress now I'm out of the mud, and upon arriving in the village I take shelter in the bus stop to take stock. I rest for a minute, eating and drinking and bracing myself for the final leg of the day. As I do so, the rain begins to ease at last and the relentless frown the sky has been wearing for the last hour or two gives way to a less threatening shade of grey. I waste no time in getting back onto the path and back into the next array of fields, skirting the hedgerows of another anonymous farm.

This time, however, the track through the fields requires me to navigate my way around a large barn full of cows. As I approach, the ground beneath my feet rapidly turns to a frothy mixture of mud and cow faeces that lays ankle deep, freshly mixed with rainwater by the churn of roving cow hooves. The herd is re-emerging from the open barn and they're stamping in and around this sea of muck. I try to carefully pick my way across what looks to be the shortest distance to dry ground, but it's intensely slippery and as I pick my way forward slowly, my boots begin to sink. Each time I try to lift my feet up, the vacuum created beneath them sucks them further in. Pretty soon I find myself completely stuck.

For a minute I just stand there and stare at my own legs, contemplating the point where they disappear beneath the surface of the cow pat slurry. I think about how it is that I find myself in these situations, and why I continue to keep putting myself through it anyway. When you're stuck ankle deep in cow shit with seemingly no good way to free yourself, it's easy to get philosophical about how you ended up there.

The cows stare at me impassively. They're unlikely to offer any assistance, but I'm at least grateful that they're not bearing down on me like an angry mob this time. I scan the surrounding landscape for any sign of a farmer who might be good enough to rescue me. Nothing. I contemplate just lying down and accepting my fate – to return to the muck from whence I came, here in this field of cows as they vacantly stare at me. Maybe it's for the best.

Eventually I decide to stop being so melodramatic and just get on with the inevitable, disgusting task of dragging myself out of this mess. I gingerly reach down and try to find a relatively dry, firm patch with my hands. It's not easy – this mixture seems to be the slipperiest substance on earth – but eventually, once my hands have submerged wrist deep, I manage to brace myself enough to force one foot out. It releases into the air with a slurping plop. I'm now hunched over, three limbs sunk into the dirt, one leg stuck up high in the air. I bring it down again carefully and try to free the next. It's like a new form of yoga, albeit a significantly less wholesome variety than the kind performed in sage scented, fern filled studios. Once both feet are free I wriggle my hands loose and try to stand up straight, but the weight redistribution causes my feet to start sinking again, so I drop back down. Then, with a sigh, I proceed to clamber on all fours like a gorilla until I reach the dry, firm grass just a few metres away beside the barn. To my eternal gratitude and relief, there is a tap built into the hedge at the edge of the field, so after wiping off the worst from my hands on the grass, I spin it onto full blast and drench my hands, legs and feet with clean water as I try not to think too hard about what I've just done.

I am tired and wet by the time I arrive in Witheridge that evening, but the fact that I'm staying in the village pub feels like a well-earned treat. Walking into the warm, glowing entrance of a pub after a day out in the elements is always welcome, but knowing that I'll be able to take off my filthy clothes, clean up, eat some food and then spend the night in a real bed is absolute luxury. After entering the front door, the landlord looks me up and down and then offers me a plastic bag to drop my mud caked shoes into so I can carry them upstairs. I also volunteer to roll my trousers up and remove my socks – there's no need to ruin his carpets. I throw my things down in the small, simple room upstairs and head straight for the shower. The warm water soothes my sore legs and washes away the accrued filth of the day, and I wonder why I ever decided that bivvying was the solution. *This* is very clearly the way to do it. Once dressed I head downstairs, order some food and grab a seat by the fire with a pint, feeling pretty pleased with a solid day's progress.

The next morning I wake up feeling fully refreshed, possibly for the first time ever on one of these walks. I head downstairs to eat a full English breakfast, with plenty of tea and orange juice to wash it all down. I pull on some fresh clothes, pack up my bags, and attempt to scrape the worst of the hardened cack off of my boots outside the front door. They're still a bit squelchy inside as I pull them on, but all things considered, I'm starting this day in pretty good condition.

Today's walk is going to be a long one. It's about eight miles to Knowstone, where I plan to have lunch, and then another seventeen miles to Simonsbath via Withypool. To make this more bearable I've found a little short-cut on the map that will bypass Withypool, cutting off five miles and bringing the total distance down to a mere twenty-one. Shortcuts feel like cheating, but there's no chance I'm going to make a twenty-six mile day – I'm still quite wary about managing twenty-one – and so I decide it's what's necessary to get me to the end. As long as I keep walking and hit all the major waypoints on the route, I see no harm in doing my own navigating over some stretches.

The walk from Witheridge to Knowstone is fairly uneventful – fields give way to trees, paths roll over the round, green hilltops and periodically rejoin the road before twisting off again on some new tangent. The whole of mid Devon repeats this pattern as it winds north; very often it's difficult to remember which stretch of rural field is which. I have arranged to meet Rupert again at the Mason's Arms in Knowstone for lunch – he's always up for a spontaneous plan, particularly if it involves food. I remember the Mason's Arms well from my previous stint camping in their garden, years back. I'm planning to make it there by midday so I'll have plenty of time to eat and rest before starting the longest leg of the entire walk.

After arriving in Knowstone I make my way into the pub. It's only just opened for the day, so I wait at the bar and politely enquire if I can see a lunch menu. The friendly lady asks me if I've booked a table, to which I reply that I'm walking the Two Moors Way and thought this would be a good place to drop in for lunch and meet a friend. There's a long pause as she considers this, before she tells me that they've been fully booked for months. Confused, I ask if there's a table outside in the garden we could sit at. Looking around towards the back of the pub, I notice the Michelin Star plaque hanging on the wall. It seems this place has changed a bit ...*

I ask if there's anywhere else in the village I might be able to get some food, or another pub not too far off the route I could maybe walk to. There's some discussion behind the bar, before the friendly lady returns and informs me that this is the last pub for miles if I'm going north. She says she'll squeeze me onto a table as long as I can order straight away, as they always do their best to accommodate walkers on the Two Moors Way. I am extremely grateful, and I grab a menu to order as fast as I can. It's a fixed price lunch menu and it all sounds

---

* Actually after a little research it turns out it really hasn't changed at all, I just wasn't paying attention the last time ...

mouth-wateringly good. Rupert hasn't arrived yet, so I order the duck for him and the lamb for myself. A member of staff brings out a small table and positions it quite near the front door, using a long bench that runs along the wall as a seat. I thank them and sit down, trying to keep the mud on my boots from messing up their nice, clean floors.

About fifteen minutes later, the pair of us are sitting hunched over this small table – me in my muddy, stinky walking gear and him in a Lego Star Wars t-shirt and a pair of old, ripped jeans – both enjoying an unexpected Michelin star lunch together. As we hastily eat, a seemingly very well heeled family park up in their Range Rover outside and saunter in demanding a table for lunch, all dressed in Barbour and tweed and a vague air of unwarranted entitlement. They get turned away for not having a reservation as we continue eating our luxury food with our heads down. We follow our first course with a cheeseboard and a pint, pay the (surprisingly reasonable) bill and hurriedly make our way back outside. We both agree that it was really good of them to cater for us without a booking, but also that we're both still very hungry.

The afternoon grows stifling and muggy as I walk down the increasingly overgrown lanes and paths towards Exmoor. This area of Devon is particularly rural; there is little sign of civilisation other than the odd cluster of farm buildings or occasional tiny hamlet. The bulk of the ridge that defines the southern border of the moor is growing ever closer, with swollen, rain-heavy clouds hovering just beyond. After an hour or so I take the shortcut I've got planned; instead of following the track onward to Hawkridge, I stick to the road as it swings west, towards a more direct ascent onto Exmoor. The real path winds up and down the valley sides over to the east and then wriggles its way along the side of the River Barle into Withypool before heading west. It takes the sting out of the climb by finding shallower ground and lengthening it over a longer distance, and it keeps away from the lanes. The way I'm choosing instead is going to be shorter as the crow flies, but will require me to ascend all the way to the top of the moor in one unbroken climb, rather than following the undulations of the valley. It's a gamble, but it's one I'm willing to take if it gets me to Simonsbath by the evening.

Eventually the route turns north and the climb begins. The lane seems to disappear upwards into a threatening wall of cloud, but I pull on the straps of my rucksack and keep pushing forward – if I can steel myself through this climb it will make for a flat and straightforward nine miles to finish up the day.

My calves and quads ache from the constant ascent. The lush foliage that's swathed the lanes in green for so long begins to give way to stark, brown, gorse studded moorland, the vanishing trees exposing me to the whims of the elements. The wind is picking up and the sky is starting to heave with vapour like a balloon ready to burst. After two miles of constant ascent, the gradient begins to flatten out and I can see the sprawl of Exmoor roll out before me, an undulating sea of rough thickets, lonesome trees and grey stone walls that run for miles. I stop by a rock and slug back some water, feeling exhausted but confident that I can make the next nine miles at a steady pace now the climb is over.

Minutes later, the rain begins – lightly at first. There's no shelter to be found this time, no bus stops, no broad, friendly oak trees. I am at the top of an exposed ridge with the wind driving at me from across the moor, over a thousand feet above sea level. The heaving skies have their eyes trained on me, but for now they're just testing the water. I push forward, hunched into my waterproof, and walk on.

An hour passes like this. I've run out of water and snacks, my legs are screaming at me to sit down and my head feels light with exhaustion. I'm fifteen miles into the day with six left to go, but the energy it took to make the ascent onto the moor has left me burned out and struggling. Night is beginning to draw in, hastened by the scornful sky and its dark, boiling clouds. All I've got to keep me going is the thought of making it to The Forest Inn tonight and then having a relatively short day's walk tomorrow to finally – at last – complete the

Two Moors Way. That thought of completion spurs me forwards, despite the protests of my limbs.

As the sun loses power behind the clouds, the dry stone wall I've been following comes to an abrupt end, and with the remaining sliver of light I can just about see the land below falling away from the top of the ridge in an unending ocean of fields and hedgerows and tiny farmsteads – all the rural delights I'd been traversing for the last two days, turning grey in the half-light. Yet that's all behind me now, I'm back up on exposed moorland and it is cold, wet, and rapidly getting darker. As I think about this, and how far I still have to go before I can eat a proper meal, my phone rings in my pocket. It's Mark calling – Mark who is of course not just my friend, but also my business partner. I immediately get a sinking feeling in the pit of my stomach. This can't be anything good.

It turns out it definitely isn't anything good. He tells me we've had a member of staff call in sick for tomorrow; no one is free to cover – including him as he's already covering for somebody else in our Torquay branch. I am immediately beyond furious. I want to scream and swear at him, or channel some of the howling wind I'm enduring down the line to reach him through the speaker. I'm too tired to rage though, so instead I mewl and complain like an upset cat, whining about useless staff and useless customers and stupid sick leave and all kinds of things I don't really mean. It's not Mark's fault of course – it's not anyone's fault – but he is on the other end of the phone and so he takes the brunt of my exhausted tantrum. I eventually hang up the phone and want to scream into the wind. I have to go home so I can go to work tomorrow. I have to go home. I can't carry on to Lynmouth.

What little energy I still had for walking has now entirely left me. The darkness is minutes away from being complete and so I trudge forward, deflated and beaten down by the elements, my weak, pathetic body, and the maddening nature of chance – all these things against me. Even though I'm using a shortcut, I am now seventeen miles into the day with five left to go before I can at last rest up – and after all that effort, all that planning, all that time that's passed since I first set out over ten years ago – and I still won't get to finish this thing. I am so angry and disappointed I want to cry.

Not long after the last of the light has gone, along with what remained of my energy, the constant threats the sky has been making at me finally get delivered – almost like it's found the exact right time to stick its boot in. The heavens open up and a deluge of cold, stinging, sideways rain pelts me from every angle. I strap my head-torch on and just keep moving, my sole motivation is now just to get off this accursed ridge and into a warm pub. Four miles to go.

The rain is so intense it's actually difficult to breathe;

the water is running down my face and into my mouth, stinging my eyes and soaking my clothes through my waterproofs. My limbs feel leaden, my head is hanging straight down and every step is an ordeal. I'm starting to really regret my decision to take this shortcut.* If I'd been on the real path, I would've been sheltered from the worst of this storm. Not only that, but I could've stopped off in Withypool and wrapped up the day there once the call came in. Instead I'm up here on the most exposed ridge in the entire world, with the full power of this malevolent sky god hellbent on destroying what's left of me. All I can do is keep pressing on. One foot in front of the other. Three miles to go.

From behind me I see headlights approaching. I haul myself into the rough scrub at the side of the lane to allow the car to pass, but instead of passing it pulls up alongside me – an old Land Rover Defender with a canvas top. The window winds down and the concerned face of a farmer stares out at me from under his flat cap. I see his mouth move but I can't hear a thing, the lashing rain and roaring engine drown out anything he may have said. I stare at him dumbly. After a second he reaches across and yanks the door handle so it swings open, shouting his offer of a lift out louder. For a split second I still consider turning him down – that same sense of staying true to the walk that I'd had outside Scorriton last year. That thought is quickly replaced by

* As Peregrine Took once said ... short cuts make long delays.

another blast of sideways rain, bringing back the still fresh grief of realising I'm not going to be able to finish tomorrow. I climb into the passenger seat and slam the door shut, thanking my saviour profusely.

I'm not in the car long – the friendly farmer only drives me a mile down the lane until I'm off the top of the weather-beaten ridge – but it's a glorious five minutes. The heater is on, I am sitting down and I'm moving forwards towards my destination at pace. No part of me feels bad about accepting this lift; every minute I spend in this car is ten minutes I don't have to spend walking face first into a pitch black rainstorm. When he drops me off a little way down the hill that descends into Simonsbath, I am more grateful than I can adequately express.

With just two miles remaining, and all of them downhill, a little of my hope is restored. Now that I'm down off the ridge the rain is still falling but the wind has subsided, taking the sting out of it. After a while spent winding downwards, the rain gives way to a swirling, dense fog that fills the valley like thick, cold soup. With only half a mile to go I turn a corner to see lights in the distance – the end is literally in sight. I am more exhausted than I can ever remember being, and the thought of sitting down and eating some proper, filling food is the only thing keeping my aching legs moving. As I reach the valley floor the fog starts to recede and through the remaining wisps of mist I can see a string of warm, glowing lamps dotted over a small stone bridge that crosses the river that rushes below. In my delirious state it's the most enchantingly beautiful sight, like something out of an epic fantasy film come to life. As I move closer, in the background of this beautiful scene I can see the sign for the Forest Inn lit up like a beacon in the darkness. I am almost overcome with emotion.

Siân greets me when I step inside. She's been waiting for me anxiously as I'm far later than I'd planned to be, and she's seen the weather go through its many awful changes. She tells me she was not too far off jumping in her car and going out to look for me. I'm just glad to see her – the soul-crushing events of the last few hours have left me in need of some looking after. We get some food together and I drink pints of water and ale – not just as part of my post-walk ritual this time, but also as a necessity to take the edge off my shredded nerves. I'm glad to be somewhere safe and warm, and happy to spend a pleasant evening in a good pub with Siân – but underneath I'm also crushed with disappointment. After all this time, and having come so close to the end – once again I'm forced to abandon the trail and head home.

WINTER

*'It's a fair climb, but I can see the top this time, and
the sky beyond shines with bright, brittle sunlight'*

IT'S DECEMBER 8TH. IT'S A COLD, bright and crisp day, and I'm in the passenger seat of Siân's little car as it zooms along the lanes of Exmoor on its way to Simonsbath. I have a stinking cold – my nose is running and my throat is scratchy, but it's no matter. This is the one remaining free day I have this year, and the weather is clear. This is my moment to finally make it to the end.

After my crushing defeat at the hands of work/life balance back in October, I genuinely thought my closest attempt yet was ruined. I knew if I wanted to I could come back sometime next year and finish it off then, but that felt like cheating – the only reason I had decided it was acceptable to complete the challenge in two sections was because I was still going to do it all before the end of the year. If I couldn't even do that then it just felt like a cop-out. Yet every weekend was booked up in November, and the chance of clear weather would grow increasingly slim as December came round.

As we drove back from The Forest Inn the morning after my autumn misadventure up on the ridge, my legs grew stiff in the car and sense of true exhaustion had washed over me. I spent the day at work, time crawling by, but my mind was still out there on the moor being lashed by the rain, trying to complete the task it had spent so long preparing itself for. Yet my body had more or less given up entirely – even getting out of my chair was a Herculean effort. I won't ever know whether I would have actually managed to walk to Lynmouth that morning; although I'd like to believe that getting up and starting straight away would've stretched my legs and shaken out the cobwebs.

Either way, I'd had to stop the fourth attempt and there was no obvious sign of a day in the calendar I might be able to finish before the year was through. Yet at the start of December, a lone Sunday opened up and the forecast looked to be clear. I made a hopeful plan with Siân that as long as the weather didn't turn too sour, we would drive to Simonsbath together early doors, and then she would drive on to Lynmouth and wait there for me to arrive that afternoon, finally having completed the walk. The week crawled by; I got sick, but the weather forecast held true. By the Saturday it seemed fortune was on my side.

Stepping out into the car park at The Forest Inn, I shoulder my small pack and get ready to go. I'm not planning on wasting any time – I know from repeated experience how fast the weather and the whims of fate can change. I knock back some cold and flu tablets with some lukewarm tea out of a broken thermos, do up the zips on my jacket for warmth, and set off. Siân toots the car horn as she sets off ahead of me, one last good luck message as I set out to finally complete the Two Moors Way.

I start walking straight away, finding the path and following it north. The bare trees lean over the boundary walls like inquisitive skeletons, and the leafy mulch on the ground carpets the track underfoot. After a short, shallow amble through the trees, the bare back of the hill rises up sharply before me again. It's a fair climb, but I can see the top this time, and the sky beyond shines with bright, brittle sunlight. The difference in the quality of light between the deep, hard blue of the summer sky and the mild, watery blue of the winter sun is remarkable. I think back to Sam's description of this leg from twelve years earlier, when he told me it was so straight-forward that even I could've managed it with my scalding trouser burn. I really hope he was being sincere.

Over the next few hours, it turns out to be entirely true. Once the track reaches the top of the hill, it skirts the edge of the east-bound Exe valley and then continues north along the long thin spindly ridge that sits between two of the many long, straight rivers that run north out of Exmoor to deposit themselves into the sea at the nearby coast. It's an easy-going walk, the track is straight and clear, only undulating slightly as it traverses the contours of the ridge top. The sky is clear and fine, I have nothing in my pack but water and snacks, and the fresh air is even clearing out my suffering sinuses. I can feel it in my bones now that I'm actually going to make it to the end, and the thought of that is beyond exciting. Twelve years of build up to this final walk – not in the way I'd planned (not that I ever did much planning), but in a few hours' time I will have finally completed the one hundred mile walk from Ivybridge to Lynmouth. I almost can't walk quickly enough; I can sense the victory in the air.

Eventually the path drops back down into the valley again, the steep sides dense with trees and the ground slick with mud underfoot. It slows me down to have to pick my way through the puddles and patches of churned up dirt, but I keep pushing forward at the best pace I can muster – I don't even want to consider what may befall me if I linger or delay. In the back of my mind there is always the possibility that I'll fall into a ditch and break a leg, or take a wrong turn and end up back on Dartmoor somehow, covered in slugs and chased by cows in the driving rain. I need to stay alert against any bit of ill fortune that may somehow derail me in this final hour of walking.

Yet nothing does. I eventually emerge from the treeline into the familiar and welcoming sight of beautiful Lynmouth. I keep walking down the road that follows the river, almost not believing my senses. I cut across the green towards the beach – I want to touch the ocean to confirm that I've actually made it. I drop my pack by the shoreline and reach down into the lapping waves. The saltwater wets the tips of my fingers.

I've finally made it to the end.

ARRIVAL

It's hard to explain the feelings that flicker around the edges of a moment like this. On paper, all I've done is reach the end of the four and a half hour walk I set out on that morning. There is no parade, no one setting off fireworks for these occasions. Thousands have achieved this before me, and likely thousands will do so again after me. The weight of feeling comes from the context we give it, a web of meaning drawn from our past and the sense of self we conjure from that. I first set out on the Two Moors Way not just today, not just in August – but more than ten years ago. I was a boy back then, a directionless boy with no plans and no thoughts other than wanting to do something spontaneous and fun with a friend. Now, however, I am a grown man with all the weight of the years that have passed behind me, providing a sense of purpose to my choices and significance to my actions that I could not have possibly perceived at all back when this began. And I know this sense of completion belongs to me and me alone. There is no parade, no fireworks. We have to draw satisfaction from our own sense of fulfilled purpose, wherever it may stem from.

The walk isn't truly complete without the ritual pint at the end, so I ring Siân and arrange to meet her at the Rising Sun, a beautiful old pub by the harbour in which I've spent plenty of time in the past. We find a warm table and order pints of local ale, staring out at the ocean as we drink them. She's been killing time while she waits because, as it's December, pretty much the entirety of tourist-driven Lynmouth is all but shut down for the winter. After drinking up we find a minute to nip into the only open shop to browse the tacky fridge magnets and buy our own bodyweight in fudge before setting off home.

As we drive back down the lanes, I go back over the whole route in my mind. It took me five and a half days in total – two nights spent in a bivvy bag on Dartmoor, two nights spent in wonderful Devon pubs, two separate cow based traumas, one slug attack, one "wrath of god" rainstorm, one accidental Michelin star lunch, two short lifts hitched. It feels longer and far more eventful than any past attempts – in part because it literally was longer, but also because I was so much more invested. In the past I'd always just tagged along in some fashion, letting things happen to me as they may. But this time it was entirely self-directed: planned and executed by me alone. And to that end, I am happy to class this as a complete success – a purpose fulfilled.

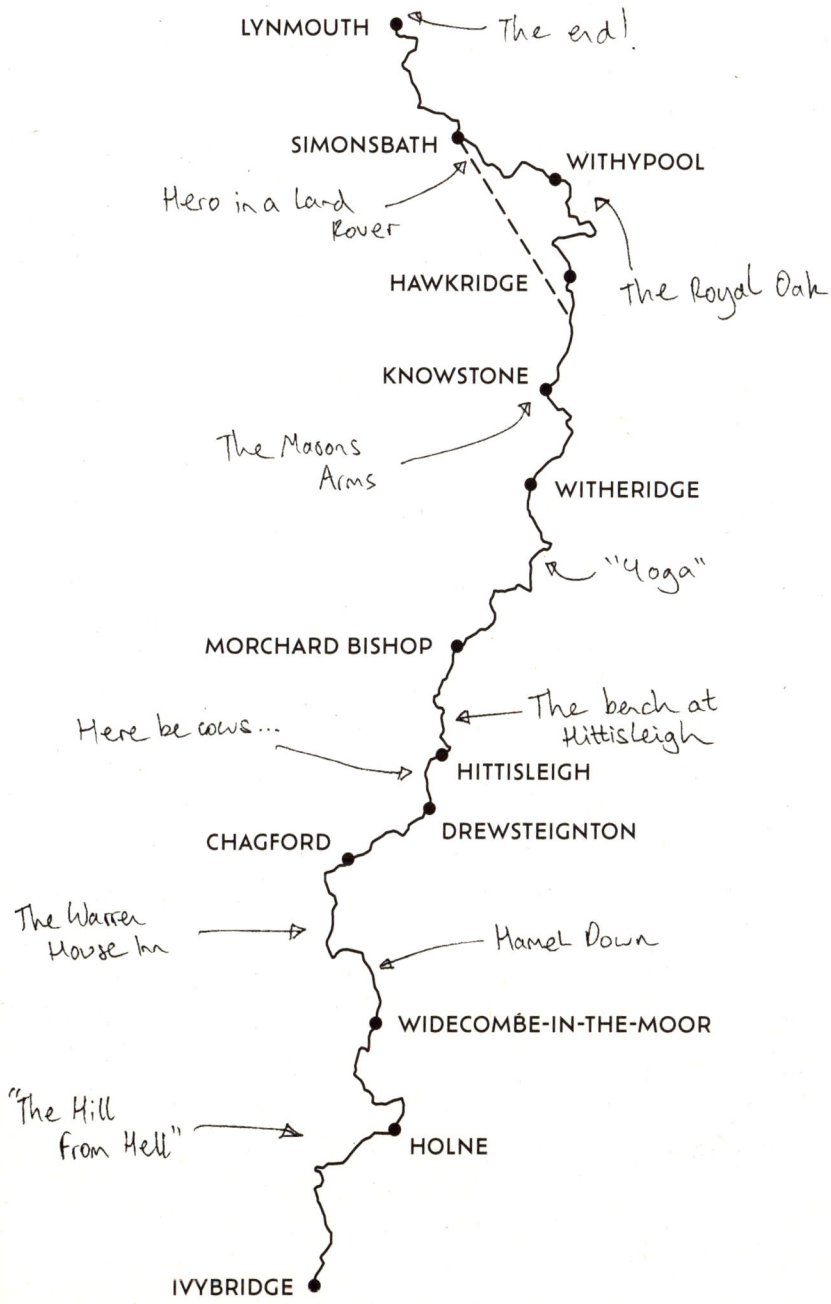

LYNMOUTH ● ↙ The end!

SIMONSBATH ● WITHYPOOL ●

Hero in a land
Rover

HAWKRIDGE
The Royal Oak ↗

KNOWSTONE ●

The Masons
Arms ↗

WITHERIDGE ●

"Yoga" ↙

MORCHARD BISHOP

The bench at
← Hittisleigh

Here be cows...
→ HITTISLEIGH

CHAGFORD ● DREWSTEIGNTON

The Warren
House Inn → Hamel Down
↙

WIDECOMBE-IN-THE-MOOR ●

"The Hill
from Hell" → HOLNE ●

IVYBRIDGE ●

ONWARD

IT'S BEEN ALMOST FOUR YEARS since I completed the Two Moors Way. I am sitting on the sofa in the living room of the house that Siân and I have recently bought together, drinking tea and staring out into the garden on a warm June afternoon. A woodpigeon is sitting like a sentry on the fence, surveying the small vegetable patch beneath him. It's a clear sunny day with a gentle breeze that rustles the tops of trees – perfect walking weather.

As achievements go, the completion of the Two Moors Way holds a strange place in my mind. I remain proud of myself for finally finishing it, seemingly against all odds; less as a feat of physical prowess, but more as a demonstration of passion and persistence and the questionable virtue of sheer bloody-mindedness. The segmented nature of that final successful attempt is not how I wanted it to ultimately transpire, so I also feel a slightly regretful sense of having had to compromise on the ideal in order to succeed.

It does serve, however, as a bookend to a particular period of my life, one spent doing impulsive, reckless, half-baked things, with little planning or preparation, just to see how they would go. The personal changes that I have undergone since I first started walking up

Butterdon Hill all those years ago with Sam, hungover and carrying a rucksack full of nothing, have turned me into someone who can now plan my time, work out my route forward, and keep going when the wild sky itself seems to want to beat me into submission.

I think back on the previous versions of myself and how they might've felt if they'd made it all the way to the end. Dressed in tatty *solar dry* trousers and sporting an impish grin, the version of me from my First Attempt couldn't have really appreciated just how momentous it all was – he started the whole thing on a whim and would've no doubt finished it with an amiable shrug, just pleased to have passed the time doing something fun with a friend. Then the version of me from the Second Attempt – one year older but absolutely no wiser – would've been excited and relieved, ready to party and celebrate and mask his obvious sadness and pain with a blur of hedonism. Although he didn't really understand any of this back then. Then later, a full ten years older, the version of me from the Third Attempt looks tired and jaded, having not properly looked after himself for a long time. In truth he never would've made it, he didn't have what it took. None of these past phantoms could've done it – they were all lacking some of the crucial ingredients that make me who I am now.

Perhaps there are other people, who – like me – need the lifeline that comes with this sense of purpose and progression, something they can fulfil over time through learning, or effort, or just relentless repetition until they reach a new, undiscovered vista in themselves. How else do we signpost growth and change in our lives?

The truth is that I am not the world's best walker. I am in no way a peak physical specimen. I am not particularly knowledgeable of maps or geography or hi-tech walking gear. All I am is a person who has grown into the challenge that was inadvertently and unknowingly laid down for them, years before when they were not yet capable of rising to it. And if anyone else needs a challenge to rise to – I'd gladly recommend walking the Two Moors Way. Lynmouth is particularly nice this time of year.

Inside the warmth of our home, I'm sitting at my desk with my laptop open in front of me. I've decided to write about my experiences on the Two Moors Way, but have yet to find a way to begin. After several fruitless false starts and abandoned opening lines, I notice that my untouched tea has gone cold, so I prepare a fresh mug and wander outside into the bright of the day. I can see the swooping valleys and iconic craggy peaks of Dartmoor off in the distance. It feels familiar and comforting.

As I stand there, an image forms in my mind – of a young man with ratty, sun bleached hair and beard, with one leg propped up on the Dartmoor National Park sign that's mounted on a granite boulder just outside Ivybridge.

I'm sure I have that photo in a drawer somewhere …

"Sam with foot on boulder"
(Photograph taken by Ben, 2006)

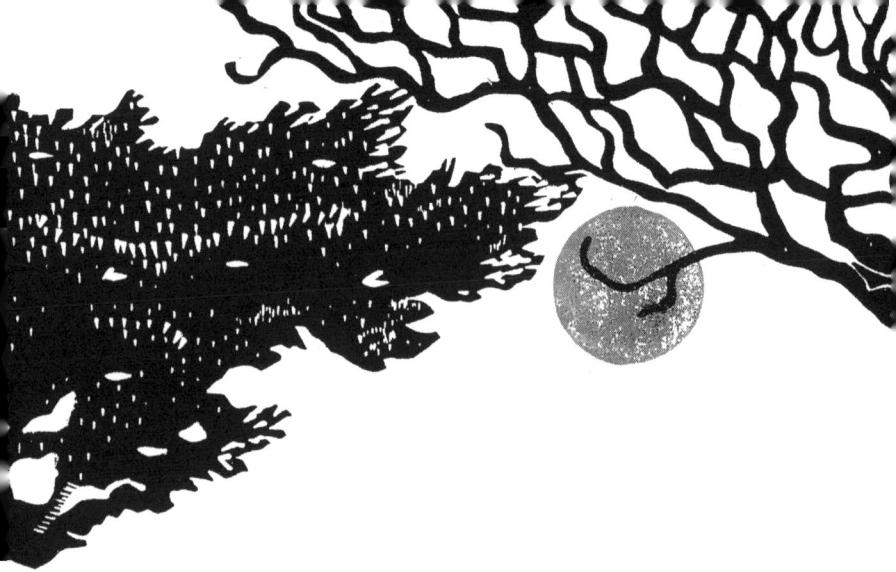

ACKNOWLEDGEMENTS

I would never have started walking the Two Moors Way without Sam Wren-Lewis.

I would never have finished walking the Two Moors Way without Mark Nicholls, Dave Reynolds, and Siân Pering.

Thanks to my family for always having my back.

Thanks to Lorna at Crumps Barn Studio for believing in this book and helping it become a reality.

Special thanks to Molly Brown for her amazing illustrations.

Lastly, I'd like to give a heartfelt thanks to everyone who has walked alongside me on this journey at some time or other – too many people to list here, but I appreciate every step taken.